Today, many of us take our rights and our government for granted. We have so long enjoyed our freedoms that we can sometimes forget the struggles that went into forging the ideals by which we now live.

As the nation celebrates the 200th birthday of the U.S. Constitution, we should all take some time to look back upon the people and the events that shaped it. For this amazing document, unique to our special way of life, is the very backbone of our rights and freedom.

THE SPIRIT OF 1787

The Making of Our Constitution

Milton Lomask

FAWCETT JUNIPER • NEW YORK

RL: VL: 8 + up
    IL: 8 + up

A Fawcett Juniper Book
Published by Ballantine Books
Copyright © 1980 by Milton Lomask

Library of Congress Catalog Card Number: 80-14654

ISBN 0-449-70262-6

This edition published by arrangement with Farrar, Straus & Giroux, Inc.

Manufactured in the United States of America

First Ballantine Books Edition: May 1987

Cover painting: *The Declaration of Independence* (detail) by John Trumbull, 1786 copyright Yale University Art Gallery

for
Kathleen Elizabeth Siebert
born August 15, 1979

CONTENTS

It should not make us love our country less to know that it was loved by those who founded it.

—IRVING BRANT IN THE PREFACE OF HIS BOOK
James Madison, The Virginia Revolutionist

PART ONE

THE CRITICAL PERIOD

1

The Crisis Ends
—and the Crisis Begins

DARKNESS HAD COME ON THAT MILD SPRING EVENING OF
Monday, March 24, 1783, and the street lamplighters of
Philadelphia, Pennsylvania, were making their rounds, each
with his blazing, sputtering, long-necked torch, when a
loud and repeated cry rent the quiet of the night.

"Peace! Peace!"

The words came from an express rider on a speeding
horse. Driving his mount up the hill from the warehouse-
jammed docks along the Delaware River, the man raced
west on Market Street as far as Seventh, where America's
largest city ended and open country began. North he clat-
tered for a short distance. Then east, down Race Street, to
the fringes of Helltown, where the shanties of a waterfront
slum silhouetted narrow, dank-smelling alleys.

Then across Second Street, up Chestnut and down Walnut, up Locust and down Spruce; past Carpenter's Hall,
where in 1774 the first Continental Congress convened.
Past the State House, where in 1776 another Continental

Congress adopted the Declaration of Independence. Past the inn where in 1781 General George Washington lingered for four months after the decisive American victory over the British at Yorktown, Virginia. Past the newest, and some said handsomest, public building in town, the Walnut Street jail, with its separate building for the accommodation of those who could not pay their debts.

"Peace! Peace!"

The news springing from the hurrying horseman's throat had reached the waterfront at dusk aboard a sailing vessel flying the flag of France. The ship's commander had picked it up thirty-six days earlier at Cadiz on the coast of Spain. He had brought it across the Atlantic as fast as heavy seas and winter storms permitted.

"Peace! Peace!"

Along the route of the shouting messenger homes and taverns emptied. Men and women piled into the street, to form into little knots, talking excitedly to one another. All of them knew the meaning of these glad tidings.

Weeks before, the Philadelphia newspapers had published a speech delivered by King George III from the throne in the House of Lords in London. "Agitatedly," according to an American merchant who witnessed the event, the King of England admitted that what only a few years back had been thirteen British colonies were now thirteen "independent states."

Seated in the chair of state, royal scepter in hand, ermine mantle draping his shoulders, right foot resting on a brocaded stool, His Majesty read from a handsome scroll held by an attendant. When the time came for him to make his historic admission, he suddenly fell silent. Almost a minute passed before he could bring himself to utter the word "independent."

He added that the statement he had just made would be written into the treaty of peace then being prepared in Paris.

Many Americans, reading the account of His Majesty's speech in their newspapers, did not believe what they read. Recent experience told them that King George did not always keep his promises. Now, with the cry of "Peace!

Peace!'' ringing through the streets of Philadelphia, it was clear that he had kept this one. His Majesty's representative in Paris had signed a treaty that declared the thirteen states in the New World to be ''free and independent.''

At last—and officially—the war of the American Revolution was over.

Peace had come.

But what kind of peace was it going to be?

Tom Paine thought he knew the answer to that question. Coming to Philadelphia on the eve of the war, this English-born master of the written word had hailed the coming of the Revolution as a heaven-sent opportunity for Americans to build in the New World a haven—''an asylum''—for all of ''the oppressed peoples of the habitable glove.'' Listening now to the cry of ''Peace! Peace!'' sounding through the streets of his adopted city, he was certain that the glorious moment he had predicted was at hand.

Tall and lean, with glowing blue eyes and a long, dangling blob of a nose, Paine had helped both to bring on the War of Independence and to win it. Unlike Washington's soldiers, he did not do these things with a gun; he did them with his pen. Again and again his music-like newspaper articles and pamphlets gave heart to America's fighting men in those dark years when many of them feared their struggle against the most powerful nation on earth would fail.

During the long, hard war, twelve stirring pamphlets fell from his pen. To each of them he gave the same title, *The American Crisis*. It was in the first of these pamphlets that Paine reminded disheartened Americans that ''the summer soldier and the sunshine patriot will, in this crisis, shrink from the service of his country; but he that stands it *now*, deserves the love and thanks of man and woman. Tyranny, like hell, is not easily conquered; yet we have this consolation with us, that the harder the conflict, the more glorious the triumph.''

After his arrival in America, Paine lived for the most part in Philadelphia. But he spent the cold months of 1782–83 with friends in Bordentown, New Jersey. Spring had come to the Quaker City when he returned there, just in time to hear the racing messenger calling out his good news on the night of Monday, March 24. Sometime during the next few weeks he cleared a space on a desk always heaped with books and newspapers and began writing his thirteenth and last *American Crisis*.

Seven years before, he had opened his first *Crisis* with a line still endlessly quoted: "These are the times that try men's souls." Now, with the cry of "Peace! Peace!" echoing in his head, he went back to the opening sentence of that first *Crisis* for the opening sentence of this last one.

"The times that tried men's souls," he told the American people in April 1783, "are over."

But they weren't.

Only the crisis called the war was over. The crisis called the peace was just beginning.

Many prominent Americans were sharply, even painfully, aware of this.

George Washington was. "It is yet to be decided," he wrote in June 1783, "whether the Revolution must ultimately be considered a blessing or a curse."

John Adams was. "From the beginning [of the Revolution]," he observed after the war ended, "I saw more difficulty from our attempts to govern ourselves than from all the armies and fleets of Europe."

Dr. Benjamin Rush was. The American Revolution was not yet over, the Philadelphia doctor told a Fourth of July gathering in 1787. "We have changed our forms of government," he added, "but it remains yet to effect a revolution in our principles, opinions and manners so as to accommodate them to the forms of government we have adopted."

The 1780's, the decade that began with the great American victory at Yorktown, was a time of troubles for the American people. It was a time of mutinies and conspiracies in the army. Of bitter arguments over the fate of the still largely unsettled parts of the country west of the Appalachian Mountains. Of struggles for power between those who were then spoken of as "the aristocrats" and those spoken of as "the lower sort" or "the common people." Of spells of economic depression. Of shortages of money. Of armed uprisings in the farmlands of New England. It was a time that has come to be thought of as the "Critical Period" of American history.

During the 1780's "a sense of anxiety" (to quote a present-day historian) filled the country. It was the anxiety of people who were beginning to fear that the goals for which they had fought the Revolution were slipping away from them.

What were those goals? The Declaration of Independence lists them. Years after the war a friend asked Thomas Jefferson what he had in mind when he wrote the Declaration. What *he* had in mind, the Virginia statesman replied, was of no importance. "All I tried to do in that document," he said, "was to express the mind of the American people."

The American people, as the Declaration shows, did not go to war in 1776 just to free themselves from Mother England's crippling tax and trade laws. Behind that long, hard conflict lay their desire to live under governments of their own making—governments that Jefferson described as resting on "the consent of the governed."

"We hold these Truths to be self-evident," he wrote in the Declaration, "that all Men are created equal, that they are endowed by their Creator with certain unalienable Rights, that among these are Life, Liberty, and the Pursuit of Happiness—That to secure these rights, Governments are instituted—That whenever any Form of Government becomes destructive of these Ends, it is the Right of the People to alter or to abolish it, and to institute new Government, laying its Foundation on such Principles . . . as to them shall seem most likely to effect their Safety and Happiness."

Life, Liberty, Safety, Happiness—and equality. Those were key words in the vocabulary of the Revolution. The American rebels usually spoke of the sort of governments they wanted, not as "democracies," but as "republics."

A democracy, in their view, was a system under which the people governed directly, all of them meeting together from time to time to make the laws and see to it that they were executed and obeyed. That kind of system, they said, might work for a New England village or even for a city as big as Boston. But it would never do for a state or nation. For such large areas the only practical government was a republic, meaning a system under which the people did not govern directly but elected certain officials to do the governing for them.

During the opening years of war, each of the thirteen states created its own republican government. In every state the people began this effort by chasing out the officials the King of England had appointed to rule them. This done, eleven states established new governments by writing constitutions. The remaining two did so by adapting to new conditions the old charters Great Britain had given them. Later these states, too, would frame constitutions.

In nearly every state a mighty squabble accompanied the making of the new government. The American Revolution has been called "two revolutions in one." While the patriots as a whole fought against England for "home rule," the people in the states fought among themselves over "who was to rule at home."

Before independence the country's aristocrats—the rich merchants and the big landowners—dominated the affairs of most colonies. But as the Revolution came on, the small farmers and the poor workers of the cities began to assert themselves, fired by the conviction that "all men are created equal."

In some states the common people won. In Pennsylvania, for example. The government established there in 1776 was one of the most democratic governments ever invented. The state constitution adopted that year extended the right to vote, previously limited to property owners, to all adult males who paid taxes. It took the political strength of the state out of the hands of the rich citizens of Philadelphia and vicinity and put it into the hands of the farmers living in the valley of the Susquehanna River and in the foothills of the mountains along the Pennsylvania frontier. The government this constitution created consisted of two principal bodies: a one-house legislature and a small Executive Council headed by an official called the president. All power lay in the legislature. Though Pennsylvanians spoke of the president of the Executive Council as their "governor," he did not have the privileges most state governors had. He could not veto the laws passed by the popularly elected legislature. All he and the other members of the council could do about those laws was make certain that they were put into effect.

In South Carolina, on the other hand, a struggle by the small farmers to run the state was unsuccessful. The wealthy rice planters who had been running it for generations continued to do so.

In New York the clash ended in a draw. There the fight lay largely between two groups—the "manor lords" of the vast estates along the eastern banks of the Hudson River and the small farmers on the other side. Some parts of New York's first constitution were what people then called "democratical." Some were "aristocratical." One democratical feature was this: a man who owned little property, or even one who owned none at all but paid a certain rent, could vote for members of the Assembly, the lower house of the state legislature. One aristocratical feature was that only rich property owners could vote for members of the Senate, the upper house of the legislature, and for the governor. This aristocratical arrangement notwithstanding, the common people triumphed in the first election. Their candidate, George Clinton, became New York's first governor. How, one may ask, could this happen since only rich property holders could vote for that officer? Easily. Wealthy Philip Schuyler, the aristocratical candidate, was a stern and haughty man, "formed for unpopularity," as one of his biographers has written. Some of his fellow manor lords disliked him and voted for Clinton. In addition, many of the small farmers on the eastern banks of the Hudson, where Clinton and his family lived, owned enough land to vote for all state officials. Small but powerfully built, shrewd and able, George Clinton would hold the governorship for twenty-one years in all.

Despite the fuss and fume over who should rule at home, the making of the state governments proceeded steadily. The Americans had some experience with this sort of thing. During the long colonial era Mother England had let them rule themselves to some extent through their state legislatures. They had reason to believe that they knew how to organize state governments. Time, to be sure, would show that some of the first governments were faulty and in need of repair, but during the early years of the war, these troubles were not foreseen. The making of the state governments was soon completed.

It was another story when the time came to invent a central or national government. To this task the Americans brought neither experience nor the knowledge that only experience can give. Every now and then, during the colonial years, the colonies had given thought to banding together under some sort of central authority. None of these attempts at union worked until 1774, when the colonies began sending delegates to Philadelphia to form the Continental Congress. Their purpose in taking this action was to install a central body whose members could speak for all thirteen colonies in their quarrel with England. When two years later the break with England came, the Continental Congress stayed on to manage the war that followed.

But the Congress was not a legal government. In theory, if not always in practice, it could do only what the states let it do. Everybody understood this. Everybody knew that a national government would have to be given some governing powers of its own. Few objected when, even as independence was declared, the delegates in Philadelphia began drafting plans for a legal national government to be known as the Confederation.

The job proved difficult. The Americans were at war against a powerful central government in England. The last thing most of them wanted was an equally powerful central government on their own soil. The only government the average American trusted was the one nearest him, the one he could get at—his state government. He looked upon a national government as a necessary evil. While the war lasted it would be needed to keep the states fighting together. After the war it would be needed to keep them from fighting one another. But the national government should have just enough force to accomplish those ends. No more. The average American wanted the bulk of the sovereignty—the bulk of the governing power—to stay exactly where it was, in the hands of his state.

The members of the Continental Congress understood this feeling. Most of them shared it. Unhurriedly, at times reluctantly, they went about the ticklish business of creating a national government strong enough to do the little that was expected of it—weak enough to be ruled by the states. The war was almost over before the Confederation came into being.

It consisted of a one-house legislature, a continuation of the Continental Congress known officially as "the United States, in Congress Assembled." It operated under America's first national constitution, a document entitled Articles of Confederation and Perpetual Union. The powers assigned to it by the states were few.

In the beginning most Americans liked this arrangement. But not all. As the new national government got underway, a few well-known men, Alexander Hamilton of New York among them, decided that the Confederation was too weak. They said it would never be able to govern a country that under the terms of the treaty of peace included almost all of what is now the United States between the Atlantic Ocean and the Mississippi River.

As the Critical Period grew more critical, complaints of this sort multipled. Nor was the discontent limited to words. Schemes and plots took form.

Some Americans said the Confederation was not working well because no republican government ever had or ever would work well. They turned to history to prove their case. History told of some little republics, established thousands of years before along the shores of the Mediterranean. None of them lasted long. In the years before the

American Revolution a few republics sprang up in the Old World, chiefly in Holland and Italy. Already these governments were showing signs of falling apart.

Those who felt no republic could work prescribed a simple cure for America's growing pains. Forget republicanism, they said. Set up a monarchy patterned after the one in Great Britain.

During the 1780's organized attempts to do just that were common. One group of schemers asked a member of one of the royal families of Europe to cross the sea and occupy an American throne. This invitation went to Prince Henry of Prussia, brother of the king of that country, Frederick the Great. Prince Henry thanked the American kingmakers for their kind offer, but said that at the age of sixty he was not up to taking on a new and difficult job.

On May 22, 1782, an Irish-born officer in the Continental Army, Colonel Lewis Nicola, broached the subject of royalty in a letter to his commander-in-chief. Nicola and some of his fellow officers were disgusted with the Confederation. They thought only a monarchy could save America. They were planning the establishment of one. Nicola suggested that the commander-in-chief take over the leadership of this effort. If it succeeded George Washington would be the first king of the United States.

George Washington's reply was brief and angry. He called the colonel's proposition "reprehensible." To another army officer, who felt the same as Nicola, he pointed out that the Americans as a whole would be happy only under a republic.

We will never know how many Americans hankered after royalty during the confusions of the Critical Period. After that era was over, after the Americans succeeded in framing a workable republic, those who had longed for monarchy preferred to forget that they had ever done so.

But they did. It is easy to see why. For a century and a half they had lived under the crowned heads of England. Battered by the political and economic uncertainties of the 1780's, some of them longed to return to the sort of rule they knew so well. That way lay safety and order.

Truly the times were troubled. By the mid-1780's articles in the newspapers, sermons from the country's pulpits, orations from its speaking platforms, letters written by its leaders—all pointed to a growing feeling that something must be done about the Confederation.

But what?

Around that question sharp divisions of opinion gathered. Around it arose a countrywide argument that continued until the Articles of Confederation were no more and the present federal Constitution stood in their place.

The political disputes of the 1780's split the people into two groups. In time these groups would acquire the names by which we speak of them today. They would come to be called the Federalists and the Antifederalists. But during much of the Critical Period more Americans than not thought of the Federalists as "nationalists" and of the Antifederalists as "anti-nationalists."

The goal of the nationalists was to convert the Confederation into what people called a "consolidated union." They wanted a government far superior in strength to the states. Indeed, some of them would like to have seen the state governments abolished, and all the political weight of the country consolidated in the national government—hence the term "consolidated union."

The anti-nationalists, on the other hand, believed that only a government like the Confederation could preserve the liberties of the people, the rights of man, for which the Revolution was fought. Many of them were willing to see the Confederation strengthened somewhat. To a man, however, they wanted no major changes in it—none, at any rate, that would rob the state governments of their supremacy.

National authority versus state authority. Nation-minded Americans versus state-minded Americans. Nationalists versus anti-nationalists. Federalists versus Antifederalists. Those phrases outline the running battle of the 1780's.

It was in the struggles of the 1780's that the American nation as we now know it was forged. The making of a nation, of course, is not a short tale to be rattled off in an idle hour. To follow the twists and turns of this one we must begin close to the beginnings of the American republic. Close, that is, to the beginnings of the war that made the nation possible.

2

The Call for a National Government

On the evening of June 6, 1776, Sam Adams of Boston, Massachusetts, then in Philadelphia as a delegate to the Continental Congress, labored long over a short letter to a friend who shared his desire to see America independent of England.

Writing was never easy for the fifty-three-year-old Bostonian who, like Tom Paine, had done more than his share to bring on the Revolution. A long-endured palsy made Sam Adams's hands tremble. His sheep-like face tightened as he struggled to find words for a letter that was harder than most to write.

He wanted his friend to know that a great thing was going to happen on the following day. But he dared not come right out and say what it was. The British authorities in Philadelphia kept an eye on letters sent by members of Congress. They might seize this one. Nothing in it, therefore, must reveal that at tomorrow's session of the Congress Richard Henry Lee of Virginia would utter treason.

15

He would say that the time had come for the thirteen American colonies to end their connection to Great Britain.

How to tell this to his patriot friend without saying it. That was Sam's problem. And this is how he did it.

"Tomorrow," he wrote, "a motion will be made, and a question I hope decided, the most important that was ever agitated in America. I have no doubt but it will be decided to *your* satisfaction."

The day dawned clear and balmy. By mid-morning Sam Adams was on his way to the Pennsylvania State House, where the Continental Congress met.

Today, visitors to Independence Hall see much the same building Sam Adams saw that morning: a gracefully shaped, red-brick structure, its two-story middle section and one-story wings standing along Chestnut Street six blocks west of the Delaware River.

In Sam Adam's day wooden posts marked where the carriageway of Chestnut Street ended and the curbless brick sidewalk in front of the State House began. Patriot Sam lowered his eyes as he entered the building, passing through a door over which the golden lion and the unicorn—the arms of the King of England—still pranced.

The first-floor hall was wide and dark and cool. On his right ranged the open arches of the west chamber, used by the Supreme Court of Pennsylvania. Sam turned to his left, into the east chamber. He now found himself in a square (forty-by-forty feet) room that looked even more spacious than it was, due to the absence of pillars under the high plaster ceiling.

Lofty windows on both sides let in the morning sun. Gray-painted panels covered the rear or eastern wall, broken at each end by a marble-faced fireplace. Centered between the fireplaces, a free-standing panel topped with a deeply carved cockleshell design provided a backdrop for the presiding officer. Visitors spoke of the highback chair in front of it as "the throne."

A few feet in from the hall door a wooden railing, called the "bar," crossed the chamber from north to south.

Sam Adams pushed through a gate in the bar to reach his place. No separate desks served the lawmakers as in today's legislative halls. The delegates sat at round tables, each covered with a coarse green cloth called baize. Sam seated himself at one of these. His tablemates this morning included his cousin John Adams and the other Massachusetts delegates except for the rich Boston merchant John Hancock. As president of the Congress Hancock occupied the "throne"—a truly majestic sight in his lavender suit, made of velvet and trimmed with gold and silver lace.

Ten in the morning was the starting hour. But on most mornings the delegates dribbled in late. President Hancock scolded, but many of them preferred to pass the morning hours in committee meetings. Others, having dropped into the rum-fragrant tavern across the street, found it hard to tear themselves away.

This morning, as the bell in the State House tower tolled ten, Hancock saw that almost all of the not quite sixty delegates were on hand. He was pleased. But not surprised. He knew what Sam Adams knew, what every man in the room knew: this was a special day.

Still, a stranger coming in at this moment would never have suspected that the "most important" question ever "agitated in America" was about to be raised. The Congress had its rules. Certain things had to be done at certain times.

Today the first order of business dealt with an incident at sea. The Continental Fleet, soon to be the Continental Navy, had seized a ship belonging to an American merchant. Considerable oratory rolled through the bright and mellow chamber before the delegates voted to return the ship to its owner.

Sam Adams fidgeted, but there was nothing he could do to hurry things along. The rules were the rules. For another twenty minutes the delegates argued over the quality of gunpowder a manufacturer had offered to sell to the Continental Army.

At last, in a room suddenly so soundless you could hear men breathe, Richard Henry Lee got to his feet.

* * *

Forty-four-year-old Lee was tall—over six feet—thin, and striking. His face was long and bony, his nose chiseled, his eyes sharp, his forehead high under a flamboyant rise of sandy red hair.

He was one of six ambitious brothers, all men of wealth and influence in Virginia. Most of them were active in politics, although only Richard Henry looked on politics as his main work. He was one of the great orators of the Congress, a spellbinder. So polished were his gestures that a friend accused him of practicing them before a mirror. Frequently, as he spoke, he poked at the air with a hand which had been maimed in a hunting accident and was now wrapped in black silk. His sentences flowed. His voice was musical. "Harmonious Lee," the other delegates called him.

When Sam Adams came south from Boston for meetings of the Congress, he usually traveled on an old horse. When Richard Henry Lee came north from his big plantation on the shores of the Potomac River, he traveled in a bright yellow coach, drawn by four high-stepping bays and attended by black slaves in shining livery. Underneath these outer differences, however, lay two minds that thought as one.

Where the Revolution was concerned both the elegant Southern patrician and the plain New England Puritan were radicals. Both saw no answer to England's oppressive laws short of open rebellion. Both were impatient with the conservatives of the Congress, who still insisted that the quarrel with the mother country could be, and should be, patched up.

Richard Henry Lee's radicalism points to interesting things about the aristocrats of his America. As the Revolution came on, many of the rich landholders and merchants in the Northern states cast their lot with Great Britain, becoming Tories. Most of those who joined hands with the patriots did so grudgingly.

It was not that they liked king and parliament so much; it was that they liked the common people of America less.

They harkened nervously to the louder and louder demands from the small farmers and the city workers for a greater share in the running of the country. In the coming of independence the Northern gentry saw a threat to its long-held position as the "ruling class."

The aristocrats did not always work together. Nor did they always agree on how things should be done. But on one point they were in accord: all believed that only those individuals who had "social authority" should be given political authority. In other words, only members of what Richard Henry Lee called the "natural aristocracy"— meaning, he said, "the few men of wealth and ability"— should be permitted to hold high government posts.

When George Clinton became the first governor of New York, his aristocratic rival for that office, General Philip Schuyler, was shocked. Schuyler admitted that Clinton was a good man, but complained in a letter to a friend that Clinton's family and connections do not entitle him to so distinguished a predominance." Schuyler's fellow patrician Gouverneur Morris saw trouble ahead for his class if the colonies freed themselves from Great Britain. "The mob begins to think and reason," Morris warned. "Poor reptiles! It [the coming of the Revolution] is to them a vernal morning . . . They bask in the sun, and ere noon they will bite."

In the South fears of this sort were heard less often. In that region owners of the big plantations standing along the Atlantic and along the navigable rivers were in charge. In recent years they had turned back more than one attempt by the poor farmers of the back country to unseat them. Most of them were now confident that even under independence they could continue to call the tune.

Under these circumstances patriotism came naturally to many Southern patricians, Richard Henry Lee among them. When he rose to his feet in the Continental Congress on that June morning in 1776, he did so as head of the delegation from Virginia. Already radical Rhode Island had declared itself independent of Great Britain. Now radical-aristocrat Lee asked the representatives of all of the colonies to approve the following motion:

> *Resolved*, That these United Colonies are, and of a right, ought to be, free and independent States, that they are absolved from all allegiance to the British Crown, and that all political connection between them and the State of Great Britain is, and ought to be, totally dissolved.

> That it is expedient forthwith to take the most effectual measures for forming foreign alliances.

> That a plan of Confederation be prepared and transmitted to the respective Colonies for their consideration and approbation.

When Lee sat down, Sam Adams got up and seconded the motion.

Lee's motion, it can be seen, consisted of three parts. The action called for by part one, an official break with England, provoked a fierce debate, but it lasted less than four weeks. On July 2, a unanimous vote for the motion as a whole carried the thirteen colonies out of the British Empire. Two days later the delegates adopted the Declaration of Independence.

Speed also marked their handling of the second part of Lee's motion, his suggestion that they seek the assistance of foreign nations "forthwith." Forthwith they did. Within the next two years three European nations would come to the aid of the Americans: France and Spain, by declaring war on Great Britain; Holland, by supplying the Americans with goods and money.

A far different time schedule awaited the action demanded by part three of Lee's motion, the creation of a national government. Sixteen months of work would go into the writing of the Articles of Confederation. Almost six years would pass before the Confederation itself took effect.

3

The Making of the Articles

Eight days after the adoption of the Declaration of Independence a thirteen-man committee laid before Congress the first draft of what were to become the Articles of Confederation and Perpetual Union. Their author was the chairman of the committee, John Dickinson.

The term "Federalist" was not yet in use, but in 1776 Dickinson's ideas of a proper national government were those the Federalists would be fighting to establish a decade hence. His draft called for a government far stronger than most of the delegates were ready to accept. During a debate that lasted the summer, they tore the Dickinson draft apart and prepared a second version of it.

On August 20, copies of the second draft were printed and distributed among the delegates. But it was never debated. During the fall of 1776 many members were absent. Dickinson himself had resigned to join the army. Those delegates still in their seats had all they could do to manage a war that was sliding from bad to hopeless.

By the opening of 1777 both situations had changed. The war was going better. Most of the delegates had returned to their seats. Even so, months were to pass before they got around to considering the Articles again.

In truth, many of them were having second thoughts about a national government. That sort of government, history told them, had a way of getting too big. It had a way of crushing the liberties of the people. No matter how carefully they wrote the Articles, what was to hinder the national government from exceeding whatever powers they gave it?

Many a delegate was beginning to wonder if a national government was worth all the bother that must be put into the making of it. After all, he already had a government—his state government. There his heart lay, and when his mind turned to the matter of a national government, awful questions buzzed and nibbled at him.

The nation struggling to be born would be hard put to survive as an island of republicanism in a worldwide sea of monarchy. If the Revolution succeeded, every king in Europe would begin living for the day when the American experiment in government by the people fell to the ground.

To deal with unfriendly monarchs the United States would need an army. That thought raised shivers. Could the national government be trusted to use its soldiers only against foreign enemies? How could it be kept from using them instead to enlarge its own influence at the expense of the people?

The central government would have to be located somewhere. No matter what state you put it in, the other states would be days or weeks away from it. In eighteenth-century America travel was slow and perilous even for people living along the Atlantic or on the larger rivers. A citizen of Charleston, South Carolina, could get to London faster than he could get to Boston. A person going from New York City to Albany by Hudson River sloop resigned himself to a journey of from six days to three weeks. What with dangerous tides lashing in from the sea and frequent spells of no wind, the ship might never get him there at all. Many a vessel, beating up or down the river, had to land its passengers short of their destination and return to its starting point.

On the best of roads stagecoaches could cover no more than thirty miles a day. In large portions of the country narrow trails raddled with rocks and tree stumps ruled out stage lines. People had to furnish their own transportation, and heaven help the traveler by land when he came to a river. Bridges were few and far between. Bad weather flooded fording sites and put ferry boats out of commission.

What if Philadelphia remained the national capital? How could the voters of New Hampshire and Georgia keep an eye on what their representatives in Congress were doing? The country was big, the interests of the people varied. Would it not be wiser to split it into two or three confederations, each with its own central government? In the 1780's Thomas Jefferson decided that, as the United States grew, it might become too large for one central government to run. If some of the states wished to separate and establish their own government, he said more than once, they should be allowed to leave the union in peace.

And money? Conducting the war was expensive. The Continental Congress was borrowing wherever it could, from foreign nations, from private Americans. Someday the ever-enlarging war debt must be paid off. Where were the dollars to come from?

Should the national government be allowed to levy and collect taxes? Never! Not even nation-minded John Dickinson dared suggest an idea so repugnant to people who had taken to the battlefield to escape the taxes demanded by Mother England.

Once the national government took over, the states would have to finance it voluntarily. Each state would have to give money to a common treasury. Should its contributions be based on the number of its people or on the value of its lands and buildings?

What an argument that question kicked up! Not on population, cried the Southern states. They said that under that arrangement their shares would be unfairly high because so many of their inhabitants were slaves. Not on property, cried the Northern states. That method would swell their payments unduly, because in their areas real-estate values were higher than they were elsewhere. Only after a long and noisy debate would the Northern states back off on this issue, permitting the contributions to be based on property.

And the sovereignty? How was that to be divided?

When the debate over the Articles resumed in April 1777, the word "sovereignty" rang out again and again. Behind it lurked the toughest question of all. Precisely how should the Articles be worded to make sure that the larger share of the sovereignty—"the reins of power," as one delegate put it—stayed in the states?

Sitting in Congress that spring was a newcomer from North Carolina, Dr. Thomas Burke. Too bad so little information about this fiery Irish-born physician and lawyer has come down to us. Even as today we call James Madison of Virginia "father of the Constitution," so in fairness ought we to call Dr. Burke "father of the Confederation."

Leaping to his feet as the debate resumed, the doctor pointed out something his fellow congressmen had overlooked. They had tinkered much with the Dickinson draft of the Articles. But the more they changed it, the more it remained the same. It still said that when the Confederation took over, the state governments would be allowed to keep only such powers as the national government did not need.

That statement, Dr. Burke said, must be turned around. The needs of the states must be put first, those of the nation second. The Articles must be rewritten from top to bottom with this thought in mind.

At this point brilliant, persuasive Dr. Burke took charge of the debate. James Wilson of Pennsylvania rose in defense of the Dickinson draft, his steady penetrating eyes round as balls behind his underslung spectacles. Gouverneur Morris rose for the same purpose, his bold and handsome face aglow with intelligence. Wilson and Morris were strong-central-government men, nationalists, Federalists-to-be. Dr. Burke's proposed changes in the Articles, Wilson and Morris argued, would reduce the Confederation to a rope of sand.

"Better a rope of sand," Burke shouted at them, "than a rope of iron."

Burke carried the majority with him. The Congress rewrote the Articles, giving them the shape they would hold throughout the life of the Confederation.

The country's first national constitution would consist of thirteen articles in all.

Article 1 gave the Confederation-to-be it's name, "the United States of America."

Other articles or parts of them outlined the makeup of the Confederation Congress—of the United States, in Congress assembled, that is. These articles told the states how to select their representatives to Congress and stated the rules under which Congress was to pass its laws.

Articles 6, 7, and 9 listed the powers of the Confederation, the things it could do. Among other things, it could declare war, make treaties and alliances with other nations, settle boundary disputes between two or more states, and borrow money.

Article 2, written by Dr. Burke, dictated the things the Confederation could not do. It did this by declaring that the Confederation could exercise *only* those powers given to it by Articles 6, 7, and 9. The Confederation could not levy or collect taxes. Nor could it regulate trade among the states. "Each state," said Article 2, "retains its sovereignty, freedom and independence, and every power, jurisdiction, and right, which is not by this confederation expressly delegated to the United States, in Congress assembled."

So ran the Articles as revised under the guidance of Dr. Burke.

In September the main British army marched into Philadelphia. The delegates fled, first to Lancaster, Pennsylvania, where they lingered only long enough—one day—to decide that they were still too close to the fighting. Then they hustled across the Susquehanna River to the little frontier town of York, Pennsylvania. There, on November 13,

1777, they gave their approval to the final draft of the Articles of Confederation and Perpetual Union.

End of the struggle to invent a national government? No. It would take another four and a half years to finish the job.

First the legislatures of all thirteen states had to ratify the Articles.

Virginia did so at once but the other states were in no hurry. For months the members of the South Carolina legislature said they would have nothing to do with the Articles until twenty-one amendments were added to them. Later the South Carolinians changed their minds and authorized their representatives in Congress to sign the Articles as written by that body.

One by one the other states did likewise. By the end of February 1779, all of them had signed except Maryland. At which point a violent argument brought the ratifying process to a long standstill.

The argument had to do with the "western lands," the vast and little known country on the far side of the Appalachian Mountains. Under colonial charters issued by England, Virginia, New York, and a few other states considered themselves owners of large slices of this territory. People called states that possessed western lands the "landed states." They spoke of those that did not as the "landless" ones. The landed states wanted to keep what they had. The landless ones wanted to see all western holdings handed over to the national government.

"The West belongs to all the people," the landless states argued. No state had a right to any of it. American soil lying beyond the accepted boundaries of the thirteen states should be given to the national government to be carved into new states as people moved in and settled it.

The problem was old. It had come up often during the long congressional debate over the Articles. A clause in the Dickinson draft would have required the landed states to hand over their western claims to the Confederation. Dr. Burke was quick to attack that instruction. Other Antifederalists were quick to support him. Out went the Dickinson land clause. In went a clause written by Richard Henry Lee, saying that no state could be forced to give up any of its ''territory for the benefit of the United States.''

There the controversy stood when, in February 1779, Maryland balked. The ''Old Line State''—so Maryland had been nicknamed owning to the unusual courage of its patriots during the war of the Revolution—declared that it would sign the Articles only when the landed states promised to abandon their claims to the West.

In the beginning, the Old Line State justified its demand by referring to a law recently passed by Congress. Under the law any soldier who served out his term of enlistment was to receive as a ''bounty'' a number of acres in the West. Each state was to supply its own soldiers with whatever bounty lands were due them.

''A fine arrangement for the Old Dominion,'' Maryland's leaders grumbled, ''but not for us.'' They spoke of Virginia as the ''Old Dominion'' because back in colonial days it was the first English possession to become a royal colony—the first to be governed, not by a commercial company, but by the king himself. Owning endless stretches of earth beyond its mountains, the Old Dominion could easily and cheaply furnish its soldiers with bounty lands. Maryland had no real estate outside its own borders. It would have to buy land to satisfy its soldiers.

Eager to see the Confederation in action, Virginia made an offer. It announced that after the war it would be happy to provide bounty lands free of charge to the soldiers of Maryland.

That should have ended the quarrel. But it didn't. For now it came to light that the officials of Maryland were not really all that worried about their fighting men. They were much more worried about their land speculators.

In eighteenth-century America a man who wanted to get rich or richer bought land in the West. Then he waited for the day when settlers came pouring across the mountains and he could sell his acres to them at a profit. It so happened that many Maryland speculators held deeds to property purchased from Indians living in the territory claimed by Virginia. It also happened that even as the rulers of the Old Dominion offered bounty lands to Maryland's soldiers, they pronounced worthless the deeds Maryland's speculators had acquired from the Indians.

Angered by this action, the Old Line State continued to hold out. The quarrel sizzled on, marked by name calling on both sides. Virginians spoke of Maryland as "M—, that Froward Hussy." Marylanders labeled their neighbor to the south "that imperial state." What most bothered the Marylanders was the knowledge that as long as the Old Dominion clung to its western lands it would grow and grow. Its influence on the affairs of the country would grow with it. The people of Maryland shuddered at the thought of joining a confederation certain in time to be dominated by "that imperial state."

Gradually the landed states gave in. First New York, then Virginia, then the others arranged to cede their western claims to the national government. Still Maryland held out. The Confederation might never have come into being had not the war forced the issue.

In January 1781 British warships began appearing in the huge bay—the Chesapeake—that divides the bulk of Maryland from its eastern shore. Frightened, the leaders of the Old Line State turned for help to the Chevalier de la Luzerne, France's minister to America. The Marylanders needed money to bolster their defenses against Britain's waterborne invaders.

France was investing millions of dollars in the American cause. It was sending fleets and armies across the sea. When the war ended, its representative in America wanted to be dealing with a single national government, not with thirteen quarreling states. Luzerne informed the leaders of Maryland that their requested loan would be forthcoming if they promised to join the Confederation. They promised.

The period that saw these developments also saw an uneasy silence fall over the battlefields of the North as the main action of the war shifted to the South. Britain removed its troops from Philadelphia. The Continental Congress was again meeting in the State House on Chestnut Street when on Thursday, March 1, 1781, the delegates from the state of Maryland signed the Articles of Confederation and Perpetual Union.

4

The Confederation
at Work and in Trouble

ON THAT FIRST DAY OF MARCH 1781—BIRTHDAY OF
the Confederation—Philadelphia celebrated. Church bells
clanged. Cannons boomed from gunboats in the river and
from the artillery post in the city itself. Parades and
speeches during the daylight hours, fireworks and candlelit
windows after dark.

Instead of gathering at the State House at ten in the
morning, the members of the Congress attended a "colla-
tion" at the home of Samuel Huntington, "President of
Congress." At two in the afternoon they gathered for another meal. This one was at the home of Samuel Huntington, "President of the United States, in Congress
assembled." Huntington owed his change of title to Maryland's ratification of the Articles just as the old bell of the
State House, which today stands cracked and mute on the
first floor of Independence Hall and is known as the Liberty
Bell, struck the hour of noon.

Two of the local newspapers called the day "memorable

in the annals of America." An orating congressman called it "a day of mortification for those infamous Tories" who for years had been saying that the Americans would never succeed in forming a central government on republican principles. That such a government now prevailed convinced the happy orator that the great aims for which the Americans were fighting were about to be fulfilled.

No such glad thoughts crossed the mind or slid from the lips of the youngest member of the Congress, twenty-nine-year-old James Madison, he who in after years would be known as "father" of the federal Constitution, which less than a decade hence would replace the Articles of Confederation.

Today a number of portraits of James Madison exist, many of them painted after he became President of the United States in 1809. From most of them he looks out at us with an expression so grim that we can only assume that whenever Madison sat for a painter he put on his public face.

He was shy. Often in large gatherings, always among people he did not know, he tended to be cold, formal. A cloud veiled his delicate features. His strongly molded mouth locked tight. A defiant scowl dulled his ordinarily bright blue eyes. People meeting him only under these circumstances got the impression he was a dry stick. Some even spoke of "the great little Madison"—he was five feet six inches tall—as "repulsive."

Those who knew him well knew better. They saw his private face, the one he displayed among people he knew and liked. In such groups Madison relaxed and twinkled. No one enjoyed a funny story more. Nobody told one better. In his student days at the College of New Jersey, now Princeton University, he was well known as a writer of droll—and bawdy—verses.

Born in 1751 he passed most of his boyhood on the four-thousand-acre tobacco plantation called Montpelier on the shores of the Rapidan River in Orange County, Virginia. He got his early education in private schools. He enrolled at Princeton in 1769 and graduated in 1771, having completed the four-year course in less than half that time.

He entered public life in 1774. First he served on the committee in charge of the war in his county, after that in the convention called to draft his state's first constitution, and after that, in the upper house of the legislature it created. While a member of the Virginia State Council, a nine-man body created by the constitution to control the acts of the governor, he encouraged and helped write the Old Dominion's agreement to turn over its western lands to the national government.

The earnestness with which he urged his state to sacrifice its territorial claims for the good of the country tells us that when Madison took his seat in the Continental Congress in March 1780 he was already a nationalist, a Federalist in the making.

Both before the Confederation became official and afterward he participated in a variety of unsuccessful efforts to give the new national government additional powers. Many of these efforts aimed at putting funds into its treasury. The Confederation could ask the states for money. It could specify the size of each state's annual contribution. But nowhere in the Articles of Confederation could Madison, or any other student of them, find so much as a sentence under which the Confederation could compel the states to pay.

Some did. Most did not. During its first twelve months the Confederation asked the states for eight million dollars. It got about four hundred thousand dollars. Rarely during the remaining years of its existence did its receipts from the states run higher than that. Most years they ran less.

Born poor, the Confederation remained poor. From rags to rags it went. Among the victims of its poverty were the country's soldiers. By 1783 many of them were serving without pay, and in the spring of that year this situation produced a rebellion in the Continental Army. Heavy with danger to the Union the episode, now known as the "Newburgh Conspiracy," gave George Washington one of the most trying hours of his long military career.

* * *

After the great American victory at Yorktown in October 1781, Washington sent the bulk of his army north to an encampment on the eastern banks of the Hudson River. He himself spent the winter months in Philadelphia, conferring with his civilian superiors in Congress.

There were many problems to discuss. Was the war over or not? American commissioners had gone to Europe in search of peace. But nobody yet knew what would come of their efforts. Some news dispatches from England said that stubborn King George was determined to keep on fighting. Others said the members of Parliament, His Majesty's bosses, were sick of the conflict and ready to give up.

Madison was one of the men Washington talked to during those winter months. Another was Robert Morris, whom the Confederation had persuaded to take over the management of its shaky monetary affairs with the title of Superintendent of Finance. People spoke of the wealthy and good-natured Philadelphia merchant, banker, and land speculator as "the Financier."

The commander-in-chief was saddened to see indications that on every side the states, once firmly united by revolutionary zeal, were now pulling apart. "I see one head gradually changing into thirteen," he noted. "I see the powers of Congress declining too fast for the consequence and respect which is due to them as the grand representative body of America, and I am fearful of the consequences."

When Washington left Philadelphia, he bore with him the feeling that unless the Confederation were greatly strengthened the goals of the Revolution could not be achieved. He also took with him orders to keep his army together until a treaty of peace was signed.

During his stay in Philadelphia the army had crossed the Hudson River. It was now encamped in the vicinity of the riverside town of Newburgh, New York.

For his own headquarters the commander-in-chief selected a house overlooking the river. It was a low-slung stone structure built in the Dutch style by two Newburgh families and known as the Hasbrouck House.

Washington was fifty years old when he moved into the Hasbrouck House. The hardships of the war had aged him. Gone were the red tints so prominent in the skin and hair of the younger Washington. The broad face with its over-large but attractively distributed features had a pale, drained look. Under the powdered wig donned for official occasions the hair was gray. Tall, about six foot three, he was still amply proportioned. Yet his 209 pounds made him slender alongside two of his top generals, Benjamin Lincoln, 240 pounds, and Henry Knox, 280 and growing.

Washington spent much of his time planning military campaigns he hoped would never take place, and which never did. British troops still occupied limited sections of the country, including New York City. Since Yorktown, however, almost no regular British soldiers had sallied forth to do battle. Such armed encounters as occurred here and there were incited by roving bands of American Tories.

Washington's soldiers were hard put to fill the days. For a time they busied themselves cutting down trees and erecting on a hill near Newburgh a large building with a vaulted ceiling that they called the Temple. Sundays its central room, big enough to hold a brigade (about four thousand men), was a church. Weekdays it was a dancing academy, canteen, or meeting hall, as circumstances directed.

Washington was tired. He would have liked to spend the cold months of 1782–83 at Mount Vernon, but he dared not leave the camp. He was afraid of what might happen there during his absence.

His soldiers were restless. They had not been paid for months. It irked them that, while their pockets remained empty, the administrative personnel of the army continued to receive their wages. In January 1783 a committee of three officers headed by Major Alexander McDougall left camp for Philadelphia. With them went a petition demanding that Congress pay its soldiers at once and set up pension plans for its officers—demands that the Confederation at that time could not afford to meet.

Washington's mail kept him abreast of the progress of this effort. He read with distress a confidential letter about it from Alexander Hamilton, now in Philadelphia as a delegate from the state of New York. He scowled over letters from another delegate, a fellow Virginian who made a point of keeping the commander-in-chief informed of what was going on in congressional circles.

These reports told him much. His own investigations at Newburgh told him more. A conspiracy was building up. If General McDougall and his committee returned to Newburgh empty-handed, they were going to try to talk their fellow officers into issuing a defiant declaration. It would call on the soldiers of the Continental Army to refuse to lay down their arms until Congress paid them—to continue functioning as an army even after the treaty of peace was signed.

Behind this scheme Washington saw the deft hand and defter mind of Robert Morris. Encouraged by Alexander Hamilton and other nationalists in Congress, the Financier was trying to get the delegates to vote and the states to accept an amendment to the Articles giving the Confederation the right to levy and collect taxes. In the distress of the army Morris and his associates saw a means of achieving their objectives. A threat by the soldiers could be counted on to force the hand of both Congress and states. Fearful as the officials of the states were of strong central government, they would look with even more fear on the prospect of their country overrun by an angry army after the war.

In his confidential letter to Washington, Hamilton said he saw no hope for the republic unless the Confederation was given the power to tax. He believed the army should "cooperate" in any movement to that end. He trusted that the commander-in-chief would agree with him.

The commander-in-chief did not agree. He was sympathetic to the financial hardships of his men. He was as eager as Hamilton to see a more powerful central government. But he quailed at the thought of his soldiers continuing after the war to function as an army. It raised in his

mind the vision of musket-toting men marching on Philadelphia, the possibility of the country's being taken over
by a military dictatorship.

In his reply to the letter from Hamilton he reminded that
brash young man that "the army is a dangerous instrument
to play with."

By the beginning of March 1783, McDougall and his
committee were back in camp and it was known that the
Congress had declared itself unable to meet their demands.
On the tenth of March two unsigned documents, later
known as "the Newburgh Addresses," were making the
rounds.

One Address described the suffering of the unpaid army.
Now that the war was ending, its anonymous author
charged, the men who had saved the country were being
deserted by the very rulers who had called on them to fight.
Congress was saying to the saviors of the nation, "Go
starve and be forgotten."

Washington was deeply moved by these words. He was
also moved by the other Address, although in a different
way. Strictly speaking, the second document was not an
Address at all. It was a notice calling on the officers of the
Continental Army to meet at the Temple on the following
day to decide what actions should be taken in view of the
inability of Congress to care for its soldiers.

As Washington's eyes fell on this notice he realized,
with a feeling of "inexpressible concern," that he was face
to face with a rebellion in his own army. Regulations forbade the officers to meet without his consent. By nightfall
another notice was making the rounds. This one bore the
signature of the commander-in-chief.

Washington pointed out that he could not sanction the
illegal meeting called for Tuesday. He proposed instead
that the officers gather at the Temple on the coming Saturday.

Rejoicing reigned among the leaders of the conspiracy
when this notice reached them. They took it to mean that
Washington would offer no objections to their schemes so
long as they proceeded in accordance with regulations.

They read with special pleasure one sentence in his call for a Saturday meeting: "The officer in rank," it read, "will be pleased to preside and report the result of the deliberations to the Commander in Chief." Did these words mean that Washington himself would not attend the meeting? Did they mean that he stood ready to go along with whatever plans were endorsed by those who did? The conspirators concluded that the words meant exactly that.

On the morning of Saturday, March 15, the officers of the Continental Army trudged up the hill to the Temple. By noon the central room was packed. Looking about, the leaders of the conspiracy were pleased to note the absence of the commander-in-chief; pleased to reflect that within the next few minutes the ranking officer present, Major General Horatio Gates—a man in tune with their plans—would step onto the platform to preside over the meeting.

But before those minutes had passed, something happened. A door at the rear of the platform opened. In the midst of a rising murmur of voices the commander-in-chief strode in.

Planting himself at the front of the platform, Washington waited for the conversation to subside. The next few minutes were not easy ones for him. For six years he had led the men sitting before him into battle with the enemy. Now, looking down into rows of frowning faces, he realized that for the first time he was about to do battle with them.

He had written down what he wanted to say. According to a journal-keeping officer in his audience, the paper in his hand shook as he began reading. He read slowly, bending toward the paper at times, giving his listeners the impression that he was having trouble reading his own handwriting. Several times he referred to the longer of the Newburgh Addresses. He spoke of the author of it as "the anonymous addresser." He recalled that the anonymous addresser had suggested that the army either move into the West and establish a separate country of its own or force Congress to grant its demands.

"My God!" Washington exclaimed. "This dreadful alternative, of either deserting our country in the extremest hour of her distress, or turning our arms against it . . . has something so shocking in it, that humanity revolts at the idea." He begged the officers to be patient, to trust their government. In time, he assured them, Congress would find ways of paying them.

The journal-keeping officer got the feeling that some of Washington's listeners were shaken by these remarks. But not many. The chill that had greeted his entrance was still present when he stuffed his prepared speech into a pocket of his coat.

But Washington had not finished. From the same pocket he drew a second piece of paper. He explained what it was—a letter from a member of Congress. It described what the delegates in Philadelphia were trying to do for the army and the problems with which they were struggling. He said he would read it, but having held the letter up, he hesitated. Men sitting in the front rows gasped at the sudden appearance on his face of an odd look. Officers in the rear bent forward, puzzled, as the commander-in-chief drew from another pocket a pair of glasses few of them had ever seen, because Washington wore them only in the privacy of his office.

"Gentlemen," he said, "you will permit me to put on my spectacles, for I have not only grown gray but almost blind in the service of my country."

That quiet statement accomplished what none of this preceding words had been able to do. It moved the officers to tears. After Washington had read the letter and left the room, and after General Gates had taken over as presiding officer, they voted to leave matters as they were and hope for the best. As the war drew near to its official close, the soldiers at Newburgh would go home quietly. They did so with nothing in their pockets but a small portion of the wages coming to them, the Financier having somehow managed to raise $750,000 so as to provide them with a little cash. For wages still due they would later receive interest-bearing IOU's, so-called public securities that the government would promise to buy back from them if and when it acquired money enough to do so.

Thus fell the Newburgh Conspiracy, but the Confederation's troubles with disgruntled soldiers were not over. Three months later troops in Philadelphia brought their demands for back wages to the very doors of the United States, in Congress assembled.

5

Mutiny in Philadelphia

THE DAY WAS A SATURDAY, JUNE 21, 1783. AT THE State House in Philadelphia both the Congress and the Executive Council of Pennsylvania were in session. Thunderstorms "accompanied by unusually high winds" had been a commonplace of the month to date. And ugly rumors were riding in on the winds.

Coming and going from the Philadelphia taverns, the Chevalier de la Luzerne, the minister from France, overheard a drumbeat of threats from the lips of militiamen belonging to the state regiments living at the local barracks. There was talk of plundering the bank, of terrifying the citizenry.

On Friday an express rider had brought to Congress disturbing news from Lancaster, campsite of the Pennsylvania Line of the Continental Army.

About eighty of the soldiers there had broken loose from their officers. Led by their sergeants, they were marching on Philadelphia, determined to settle their accounts with Congress, by words if possible, by guns if words failed.

Thus began a comic-opera mutiny, important only as another symptom of the ills from which the country's national government was suffering.

By Friday evening the Continentals from Lancaster had arrived and had joined forces with the state troops at the Philadelphia barracks. Shortly after Congress met the next morning, some five hundred soldiers surrounded the State House. Threats and oaths filled the air. Some of the mutineers broke windows and poked their bayonets inside. The proprietor of the tavern across Chestnut Street came beaming over, bringing free drinks for the noisily milling soldiers. As wine and rum slid down thirsty throats, more and louder threats and curses flew out of them.

Delegate Hamilton hastened to the meeting room of the Executive Council of Pennsylvania. President of this body—chief executive officer of the state—was John Dickinson, solemn as ever on the outside, inwardly rather pleased at the plight of a Congress that could have handled this situation had *his* Articles of Confederation been accepted instead of those inspired by Dr. Burke.

Hamilton demanded that Dickinson summon the militia to protect the representatives of the United States of America. Dickinson took him to a window, pointed out. Hamilton got the idea at once. The militia was already there, screaming, brandishing bayonets, and getting drunk.

Dickinson did agree to summon the ranking military officer of the state. Major General Arthur St. Clair, duly summoned, hurried out to speak to the mutineers. They told him to go back where he came from. He did, and Hamilton returned to the meeting hall of the Congress to report that the executive officer of Pennsylvania could do nothing to help.

At three o'clock the Congress voted to adjourn. Most of the delegates departed by way of the State House yard. This large treeless area stretched from the rear of the building to Walnut Street. A brick fence, seven feet high, enclosed it.

As the delegates stepped into the yard, the soldiers poured into it, almost filling it. Jeers and taunts echoed from the walls. There were threatening gestures, bellowed insults. But little by little the mutineers drew to either side, leaving path enough for the scowling congressmen to pass through and out by the Walnut Street gate.

That evening the mutineers roared about town. There was some damage. Not much. Philadelphia had seen worse. Congress met for a special candlelit session. The lawmakers remained together only long enough to decide to leave a state whose authority had proved unable (or was it unwilling?) to protect them in their hour of need.

With this action the Confederation Congress became a nomad. It would wander for the rest of its days. It met next at Princeton, New Jersey. After that at Annapolis, Maryland. After that at Trenton, New Jersey. Finally in New York City.

6

Panic at Annapolis

Wherever the Congress went, its troubles followed.

Lack of money continued to crown the list. As keeper of the Confederation's coffers, Robert Morris did his best, and his best was good. Even those aware that the merchant-banker-speculator was using his position to fatten his own already ample fortune admitted that his ability to keep the Confederation going on an empty purse was miraculous. "The Financier has his hands full," someone remarked to George Washington. "If only," said Washington with a sigh, "he had his pockets full."

Many attempts were made to pass laws that would give the Confederation more revenue. None passed. Many of the states were willing to go along with the idea but only on the condition that all of the others went along with it, too. Getting some of the states to agree on something was possible; getting all of them to agree on anything, impossible.

Efforts to strengthen the Confederation by amending the

Articles met the same fate. A clause in the Articles themselves forbade any addition to them unless all thirteen states consented to it.

The Confederation's inability to regulate trade among the states set them to fighting with one another.

New York had one of the finest seaports in the world. New Jersey and Connecticut had none. Jersey citizens receiving foreign goods coming in through the port of New York City had to pay duty on them to New York State. One prominent Jerseyite was heard to say that "our neighbor state's practice of making us pay for goods moving across its harbor is not a neighborly way to behave." If Governor George Clinton of New York learned about that remark, he chuckled. New York citizens paid almost no taxes. The duties collected from New Jersey and Connecticut paid most of the expenses of the New York State government. Somebody in New Jersey or Connecticut should have complained about "taxation without representation." Perhaps somebody did.

During the 1780's hard money—silver and gold—was scarce in all parts of America, invisible in some parts. The Articles permitted the Confederation to coin hard money, but it never did. It couldn't. As the old saying goes, it takes money to make money and the Confederation had none to make it with. What little hard money was around consisted of English sovereigns, French *louis d'ors*, Spanish *pistoles*, and other coins sent to America by foreigners in exchange for American goods. In no two states did the dealers in goods give the same value to foreign coins. Consequently a killing amount of work—and irritation—went into the settling of accounts between Americans trading with one another across state boundaries.

It was a rare farmer living back from the seacoast who ever laid eyes on a sovereign or a *louis d'or*. When he went into town to buy seed or equipment, he found himself at the mercy of the city slicker. If the merchant was willing to accept the farmer's grain in lieu of money, fine. If not, the farmer had to go into debt. If his efforts to get money to pay the debt failed, he lost his farm.

Some states tried to ease these problems by fixing prices

or by issuing paper money. Price fixing seldom worked, and the paper money helped only a little and up to a point. One point beyond which it did more harm than good was the state line. A merchant living in State A simply turned up his nose when people from State B tried to buy his goods with paper money issued by their state. Ill will flourished. Much of it came from the determination of each state to keep what it had within its boundaries. Sometimes the legislature of a state, seeing its citizens spending money elsewhere, rushed through a law aimed at discouraging them from doing so. When one state passed such a law, adjoining states sometimes retaliated by doing the same. When this happened, a bad time was had by all.

In 1783 James Madison ended his first term in the Congress and went home. He would be back later. Meanwhile, watching events from Virginia, he grieved at ever-increasing signs of disrespect for the Congress.

Back in the early days of the war, the states made a point of sending their best men to the national legislature. By 1783 this was no longer true. Many good men still sat there, but of those coming in, more and more were second-stringers.

Many capable men were no longer interested in the Confederation. They preferred to serve in the governments of their states. That, in their opinion, was where the important things were happening. Appointed to Congress by their legislatures, some highly respected men refused to go. Others went reluctantly. Named to Congress shortly after its move to Princeton, one prominent Southerner let it be known that he did not look forward to spending the coming year "in the capital of a foreign land."

Even before the lawmakers left Philadelphia, absenteeism had set in. After they left, it worsened. In some states the legislatures were slow about electing delegates. In other states the legislatures, having named delegates, were slow about raising money to send them to wherever the roaming Congress happened to be. The election to Congress was an annual event. In some years some legislatures never got around to holding one at all.

These practices made it hard for the Congress to do its job. Often for weeks on end so few delegates were on hand that all they could do was assemble in the morning, count noses, chat with one another for a while, and vote to adjourn. For lack of delegates to turn them into laws, badly needed bills gathered dust on the desk of Charles Thomson, the secretary for the Congress.

Even when enough representatives were present, passing laws was like running an obstacle course. The Articles of Confederation made it so. Each state had one vote, but it could cast it only if at least two of the state's delegates were on hand. Most laws required the approval of seven states. Important ones, those dealing with financial or military matters, required the approval of nine.

Treaties made with foreign governments fell into the category of important laws, and in the winter of 1783 the arrival of the "definitive" or final treaty of peace tumbled Congress into a dismaying experience.

Labeled "preliminary," the treaty hawked through the streets of Philadelphia in the spring of 1783 ended hostilities between America and England. But it did not end a war that began as a simple colonial rebellion, only to widen enormously later on.

During its closing years the War of American Independence became what today we call a world war. Three of Great Britain's enemies in Europe—France, Spain, and Holland—either entered the conflict of their own volition or were drawn into it. Signed in Paris on January 20, 1783, the preliminary treaty settled scores between the United States and England. Seven months went by, however, before the disputes of interest to all the battling nations were settled with the signing in Paris on September 2, 1783, of the final treaty.

The national legislators were meeting in the prayer room of Nassau Hall, the college building at Princeton, when the news of this event reached them on the last day of October. They were meeting in the square, classically designed senate chamber of the Maryland State House in Annapolis when the treaty itself came before them. At this point—November 26—all they had to do to make the peace final and forever was to ratify the document now in their hands.

But weeks later the definitive treaty of peace was still lying on Secretary Thomson's desk—unratified! No treaty could take effect until nine states approved of it, and in the last month of 1783 only seven states were fully represented on the floor of the Congress. One delegate each from two more states was in attendance, but neither of them could vote on the treaty until at least one more delegate came along from his state. To make matters worse, Eleazer McComb, one of the two on hand from Delaware, was muttering about the "tangled condition" of his "private affairs" at home and threatening to leave Annapolis at any moment.

What to do? In a letter to Edmund Randolph of Virginia, the tall, gangling red-headed delegate from that state, Thomas Jefferson, described in detail the mess in which the Congress found itself. The whole world was waiting for the United States of America to ratify the definitive treaty of peace, and for the time being the United States was powerless to do so.

In his letter to Randolph, Jefferson spoke with concern of a clause of the treaty which stated that the ratified agreement must be back in Paris no later than the third of March. Jefferson's letter was dated December 16. The day on which the treaty must reach Paris lay less than three months away. On the rough seas of winter the sleekest of sailing ships would need at least a month and a half to get it to Europe.

Suppose the ratified document arrived in Paris after the deadline date? It was common knowledge that powerful personages in England did not like the treaty. They thought king and parliament had given the United States too much land in the New World. They frowned on a section of the agreement that allowed the Americans to take fish from the Atlantic off the coast of British-owned Canada. If the treaty failed to reach Paris in time, would Great Britain use that small technical violation as an excuse to tear it up and replace it by one less advantageous to the United States?

Time would prove Jefferson's worries groundless, but in

those hectic closing weeks of 1783 nobody in Congress could foresee that this would be the case. All through December a pall of panic hung over the high-ceilinged Maryland senate chamber, with its gently sloping visitors' gallery and tall small-paned windows.

Toward the end of the month, express riders hired by the Congress fanned out to the five states which had only one representative on the floor, or none at all. To each of them went the same message. "Hurry your delegates to Congress," it said in effect. "The treaty for which so many Americans have fought and died must be signed at once. The honor of the Republic is at stake."

Slowly the answers came back. His Excellency George Clinton, governor of New York, regretted to say that his state had not got around to choosing delegates for the year. Nor had it any plans to do so. What Clinton seemed to be saying was that the Empire State had better things to do than send men to Congress. New Hampshire's reply said the same thing. Georgia wrote that it had selected delegates but none of them was planning to leave for Annapolis until spring. That left only Connecticut and New Jersey, both of whom wrote that they had named delegates and hoped to get them on the road soon. But neither could say when "soon" would be.

The old year ended. The new one began. The definitive treaty of peace still lay unratified on Secretary Thomson's desk.

Delegate Cadwalader Morris of Pennsylvania proposed that the men from the seven fully represented states sign the treaty and send it off. Perhaps Great Britain would never notice that the ratification was incomplete. Jefferson objected. Just because England had lost the war didn't mean it had lost its wits. England's peace commissioners in Paris knew what was in the Articles of Confederation. They would see at once that the treaty was not legally ratified. The worried Virginian offered what he thought a better idea: send the treaty off with the signatures of the seven states on it. But send with it a note saying that the signatures of two more states would follow as soon as they could be obtained.

Neither this proposition nor that of Cadwalader Morris went beyond talk. Other talk centered on South Carolina. One of that state's delegates, Ralph Izard, was present. Another, Richard Beresford, had left home but had fallen ill en route to Annapolis. Word that Beresford was now confined to a bed in one of the inns of Philadelphia prompted a delegate to suggest that the lawmakers adjourn to that city and meet for one day in Beresford's sickroom. That way the necessary signatures of South Carolina could be added to the treaty.

Consideration was being given this proposal when on February 13 two delegates from Connecticut walked into the senate chamber of the Maryland State House. Early the next morning Beresford walked in, recovered from his illness.

That day the United States ratified the treaty.

Eighteen days now remained in which to get it to Paris by the March 3 deadline. The delegates took no chances. They had three copies printed. They ordered three messengers to carry them to Europe on different ships. Whoever got there first was to deliver his copy to the peace commissioners in Paris.

All three were late. The treaty reached Paris a month past deadline. But England raised no objections. On April 3, 1784, in a ceremony known as the exchange of instruments of ratification, the definitive treaty of peace became official.

The Confederation had weathered another embarrassment. But the cause of it—absenteeism—lingered on. There would be days in the future when only ten delegates answered the morning roll call, many days when so few states were fully represented on the floor that no legislation could be passed.

7

The Critical Year

1786 WAS THE CRITICAL YEAR OF THE CRITICAL PERIOD.

By the opening of that year the Confederation had collapsed for all practical purposes.

Every thinking American knew it had. But except for a handful of unwavering nationalists like Madison and Hamilton, few of the country's leaders were ready to support the still occasionally offered suggestions for bringing back to health a Congress that was mortally ill. Fear of strong central government—the very feeling that had made the Confederation the puny thing it was—still directed the thinking of more Americans than not.

Among the few strong-central-government men sitting in the Congress in 1786 was twenty-eight-year-old Charles Pinckney of South Carolina. Handsome in a sardonic way, dapper, brilliant, and arrogant, young Pinckney was often on his feet, listing in his clipped speech the troubles of the country. Everywhere he looked, he saw one state fighting over commercial matters with other states. In state after state the legislatures were pouring out unjust laws, laws that enriched some of their citizens at the expense of others. Everywhere state governments, created to keep order and give every citizen an equal chance at his heart's desire, were coping instead with a democracy gone so wild that it looked like anarchy. The goals of the Revolution were not being realized. The "American Republics"—the thirteen state governments—were "headed for destruction."

Most of Pinckney's fellow delegates agreed with his bleak picture of what was happening to the country. But almost none of them went along with his statement that the answer to the problem was to reform the Confederation. Give the national government the additional powers it required, Pinckney said in his hurrying voice, and all will be well.

In May he rose in the Congress—then meeting in New York City—to offer a motion. He suggested that the Congress take time out from its other work to consider "the state of the union." He predicted that the members would find the country to be in peril. He expressed the hope that they would ask the states to hold a convention for the purpose of revising the Articles of Confederation.

The delegates did examine the state of the Union. They did find it bad. But they refused to ask the states to call a constitutional convention.

Objections to that action exploded on all sides. A constitutional convention indeed! Who knew what the men sent to such a convention would do? Every new power they gave to the national government would have to be taken from the states. Where would that leave the states? Perhaps the members of the convention would limit themselves to those few revisions of the Articles that nearly everyone thought necessary. Perhaps they wouldn't. Perhaps they would go off on some tack of their own. They might recommend the establishment of an entirely different kind of national government. They might end up saddling the country with "a baleful aristocracy." With a monarchy masquerading as a democracy. With a despotism, under which the liberties of the people would wither away.

As Congress thought in May 1786, so thought most of the country's leading citizens. At any rate, so thought most of those who went to the trouble of making their opinions known in articles written for the newspapers. Or in letters to friends. Or in speeches from pulpit or other public platform.

"Our body politic is dangerously sick." So Patrick Henry of Virginia concluded in 1780. By 1786 many other well-known Americans had reached the same conclusion.

Sam Adams had. Sam was no longer sitting in the Congress. He was watching events from his home in Boston. Sam remembered the spirit of 1776. Remembered it well, for no one man in the country had done more to fan the coals of rebellion. He remembered those years on the eve of the war when Americans the country over stood ready to give everything they had, including their lives, to shake off the yoke of crown and parliament.

He remembered that rainy winter night when at his bidding and under his direction Boston citizens disguised as Indians marched to the city docks, boarded three little ships, and dumped fifty thousand dollars' worth of English tea into the bay. What a magnificent rebuke to tyranny that action was! "Bold . . . daring . . . firm, intrepid and inflexible . . . an epocha in history." So Cousin John Adams described the Boston Tea Party of December 16, 1773.

But now it was 1786, and when Sam Adams looked around, what did he see? He saw the mincing movements and haughty stares of the members of the Boston Tea Assembly, a club but recently founded for the purpose of promoting "decent manners and polite attentions." From the glory of the Tea Party to the pomp and circumstance of the Tea Assembly—thus "in a few short years," said unhappy Sam Adams, have the American people "*declined*." In Sam's eyes the existence of the Tea Assembly was but one of many examples of the growing passion among the American people for pleasure and dissipation, for "etiquette and LUXURY." For living in a "stile" far higher than most of them could afford. For elegant homes and sumptuous carriages.

Sam mourned. In years past he had given his all to help bring on the Revolution, for one reason only. Only by breaking with England could the virtuous Americans separate themselves from the wicked English. Now the revelation that many of his countrymen were wicked, too, left Sam Adams sick at heart. Looking ahead, he saw the naked claws of catastrophe. Republican government could survive only in a country where the people were virtuous. Such was Sam Adams's firm conviction. In a republic, he reasoned, it was the people who decided who was to run the country, and bad citizens could not be expected to elect good ones to office.

Sam could be expected to think in these terms because he was a Puritan: a believer in plain living, a believer that sin is real, that it is all around us, and that the human being's main duty is to do battle against it. But in all parts of the country other men, some also Puritans but most of them not, were saying what Sam was saying in different ways. Richard Henry Lee, that luxury-loving prince of Southern cavaliers, had agreed with Sam Adams many times in the past. He agreed with him now. "A corrupted people and republicanism," Lee asserted, could not "coexist."

"Virtue," a group of New Hampshire ministers pointed out, was helpful "to any kind of government, but it was absolutely necessary to the existence of a republic." In a republic, one of them declared, "the people are not only the source of authority; but the exercise of it is in a great measure lodged in their hands. Corruption therefore among the people at large must be immediately felt and if not seasonably prevented proves fatal in the end."

"I myself have been an advocate for a Government free as air," said Rufus King of Massachusetts, brilliant Harvard-trained lawyer and statesman. But, he added, "my

Opinions have been established upon the belief that my countrymen were . . . governed by a sense of Right and Wrong. I have ever feared that if our Republican Governments were subverted, it would be by the influence of commerce and the progress of luxury. But if in opposition to these Sentiments the great Body of the people are without Virtue, and not governed by any internal Restraints of Conscience, there is . . . room to fear that the Framers of our constitutions and laws have proceeded on principles that do not exist, and that America, which the Friends of Freedom have looked to as an Asylum when persecuted, will not afford that Refuge.''

John Dickinson had long since declared that mankind falls into two large classes: ''the licentious and the worthy.'' By 1786 many thoughtful Americans had decided that the ''licentious'' had taken charge of the country and were ruining it.

Having put their finger on what seemed to be America's sickness—a largely licentious citizenry—the critics of society were quick to suggest what seemed to be the only possible cure. That, they said, was ''governmental reform.'' Only a morally strong people could thrive under weak governments, under what Rufus King called ''Government free as air.'' Since many Americans had turned out to be something less than angels, the time had come to construct ''stronger governments.''

Be it noted that the critics of the country did not say ''government.'' They said ''governments.'' Those who wanted ''governmental reform'' in early 1786 were not thinking about the national government. After all, the real political power of the country was not lodged in the Confederation. The Confederation was weak. The states in their wisdom had made it so, and so it should remain. The real power of the country lay with the states. It was the state governments, therefore, that should be reformed.

Those who voiced this view liked to remind their listeners of the circumstances under which the state governments were created during the early years of the war. Haste marked the process in every state. Consequently, mistakes were made.

Fresh in the minds of the makers of the first state governments were the sufferings that the American people had endured at the hands of the oppressive royal governors whom the kings of England sent across the sea to rule them. Prodded by this experience, the makers of the state constitutions put most of the ruling power in the hands of the people's elected representatives (the legislature) and as little as possible in the hands of the governors. In most states the governor's power to veto a law was severely limited. In New York State, for example, the veto power belonged to a five-man body known as the Council of Revision. Of this body Governor Clinton was only one member with only one vote. The other members were state senators, elected to the council by the larger and more popular lower house of the New York legislature.

Let the people's elected representative run the show, the early constitution makers reasoned, and freedom will prevail. But by 1786 just about everybody had learned that legislators free to pass any old law—with no governors or courts to check them—could be as tyrannical as royal governors appointed by a distant monarch.

In state after state the legislatures were pouring out laws so fast no one could keep up with them. Some laws contradicted other laws. Many were unjust. Some trampled on the rights of the poor, some on the rights of the rich. To make matters worse, the turnover of members was enormous. At the beginning of every year in Virginia, for example, almost half the men sitting in the legislature were men who had not been sitting there the year before. Back in the war days a frequently shouted slogan was "Tyranny and King George!" Now a frequently and angrily shouted slogan was "Tyranny and the Legislature!"

The American republics—the state governments—had become too democratic. It followed, said the advocates of reform, that they should be made less democratic.

So most Americans were thinking in the opening months of 1786. But in the remaining months of that year a stunning change took place. The demand for governmental reform continued to be as strong as ever—but the focus of it shifted.

"Reform the state governments and our troubles will go." That was the prevailing cry of the American people in the opening months of the critical year of the Critical Period. "Reform the NATIONAL government and our troubles will go." That was the cry when 1786 ended and the new year began.

"Our sufferings," a 1787 Fourth of July orator told his Massachusetts audience, "have arisen from a *deeper foundation* than the deficiency of a single constitution." Even if Massachusetts had a perfect government, he said, its citizens would still be plagued by troubles "should our *National Independence* remain deprived of its proper *federal authority*."

Here was the voice of Federalism rising in a land that only a year before had been almost entirely Antifederalist.

So swift was the change in public opinion during 1786 that historians tend to disagree as to which of the three larger developments of that year brought it about.

Was it the ferocious battle of words on the floor of the Congress over the Jay-Gardoqui treaty negotiations?

Was it the action—the daring action—of a few nation-minded men in the closing hours of the Annapolis Convention?

Was it the armed outbreak in rural New England known to us as Shays's Rebellion?

Or was it—as logic suggests—all three?

8

The Nationalists Take Charge

THE QUARREL IN CONGRESS OVER THE JAY-GARDOQUI negotiations was an outgrowth of the efforts of the new republic to deal with its economic difficulties. Great wars tend to be followed by the spells of hard times we call economic depressions. The Revolutionary War was no exception. All through the 1780's such depressions came and went.

Most Americans took them in stride. They knew that the country they had won the right to call their own was rich in resources. Rich in timber that could be felled and made into ships for sale to other countries desperate for ships for use by their naval and trading fleets. Rich in minerals, waiting to be taken from the earth and converted into a thousand useful things. Rich in offshore waters teeming with cod and mackerel, bass and lobster. Rich in soils capable of yielding uncountable pounds of tobacco and bushels of corn. Before the war British law discouraged the erection of factories on colonial soil. But now the Americans could do what they wished, and everywhere the factories were beginning to spring up. However poor they might be today, the Americans of the 1780's could look forward to richer tomorrows. Meanwhile, the present must be taken care of. And then as now Americans looked kindly on governments capable of helping them make their livings—and unkindly on those that lacked that capability.

In the 1780's the material welfare of the republic hinged on its trade with other nations. Almost the only markets for the things Americans grew—lumber, rice, and tobacco, for example—were in Europe. Pending the completion of enough factories, most of the things they needed—clothing and furniture, for example—had to be purchased from Europe.

There were profits to be made from this waterborne commerce. But what the Americans got out of it depended on the ability of the Confederation to negotiate trade agreements—so-called treaties of commerce and amity—with foreign countries. The Articles of Confederation gave Congress the power to make such treaties. But by 1784 an upsetting fact had become apparent: having the power was one thing, exercising it was another.

By that date America had obtained trade agreements with a few countries. But from that date on, almost all the Confederation's requests for trade treaties were turned down because it had become clear that the new republic could not pay its debts.

After the war, as before, Americans sold more goods to England and bought more goods from England than it sold to or bought from any other country. But when American diplomats proposed that England and the United States negotiate a treaty of commerce and amity, King George said nothing doing. In a letter to his prime minister the King revealed the reason for this brusque refusal. "That revolted state," he said of the United States, "certainly for years cannot establish a stable government."

One European country did not take this attitude. In 1785 the kingdom of Spain sent across the sea an able and experienced diplomat named Diego de Gardoqui. Gardoqui's instructions were to get together with the American Superintendent of Foreign Affairs, John Jay of New York. He and Jay were to draft a trade agreement between their two countries.

Up and down the Atlantic coast American businessmen waited eagerly for Jay and Gardoqui to complete their work. They looked forward to the day when Congress, having examined the proposed agreement, voted to accept it. Once the treaty took effect, the plantation owners of the South could count on selling more rice and tobacco to Spain itself and to Spain's far-flung colonies in the New World. Northern merchants could count on selling more timber to Spanish shipbuilders. Both the Southern planters and the Northern merchants liked trading with Spain. That country usually paid for what it bought with hard money—with those precious gold and silver coins that were so hard to come by in the America of the 1780's.

Eagerly they awaited the arrival of the proposed treaty on the floor of the Congress. But great was their chagrin when in the spring of 1786 it finally got there. For the agreement that Jay and Gardoqui had written turned out to have a string attached to it.

It was a long string. It stretched across the United States right to its western border, the Mississippi River.

In the 1780's almost all of what is now the United States on the far side of the great river belonged to Spain. Spain, therefore, controlled the river. From that fact dangled the string. Spain stood ready to sign the treaty only on one condition: the Americans now settling the new republic's western lands must promise to make no effort for the next thirty years to use the Mississippi River for shipping the products to market. They had the shipping lanes of the Atlantic at their doorsteps.

But the delegates from the five Southern states were horrified. Many former inhabitants of their region had climbed across the mountains and were now living in the West. A growing West spelled a more prosperous and more influential South. Forbid the farmers of the frontier to use the Mississippi and immigration into the West might stop.

Even more dreadful things could happen. The settlers already living in what are now Kentucky and Tennessee might rebel. They could not afford to ship the things they grew on their farms across the mountains. The great river was their only route to market. Angry at the Confederation's failure to protect their interests, they might secede from the United States and establish a separate country of their own. Worse yet, they might transfer their allegiance to Spain in return for the right to use the Mississippi.

The debate in Congress was the sharpest the country had yet seen. It was North versus South. It gave the Americans a foretaste of the even harsher split that a few decades later would pitch them into the Civil War.

It took nine states to ratify a treaty. Maryland, Virginia, North Carolina, South Carolina, and Georgia (the five Southern states) never wavered in their opposition to an agreement that would close the Mississippi to American use. Consequently, the treaty drafted by Jay and Gardoqui was doomed from the start. But the treaty was so desperately needed and feelings about the Mississippi questions ran so high that the debate raged for many months. After it ended and all hopes for a treaty disappeared, the people all over the country would spend many more months trying to figure out the meaning of what had happened.

Many of them began wondering about things they had given little thought to before. Was reform of the state governments the only way to correct the problems of the country? Were they looking in the right direction? Was it possible that, instead of looking only at their state governments, they ought to be looking at least as hard if not harder at their national government? Obviously only a much-strengthened national government could provide the republic with treaties favorable to everybody, whether they lived in the North or in the South.

Yes, in the summer of 1786 the Americans had much to think about. And while they were mulling over the lessons learned from the debate over the Jay-Gardoqui treaty negotiations, other events arose to cause them further thought.

* * *

We know now what came of the convention in Annapolis, Maryland, in the fall of 1786. It proved to be the preface, the prelude, the stepping-stone to the Federal Convention in Philadelphia that during the coming summer would frame the second and present constitution of the United States.

It is easy to suppose that when, in the spring of 1786, James Madison set out to bring about the Annapolis Convention, he knew what it would lead to. But he didn't. Had he known, he would have put on his relaxed private face, trotted out the funniest story he knew, and danced in the streets. For by 1786 Madison had come to the great decision that would dictate his political actions for the remainder of the decade.

For many years this small and unexciting-looking man had thought that, with a few amendments, the Articles of Confederation might be made to work. Now he knew better. He knew that no amount of tinkering could save the Confederation. It was done for. The time had come to give it a respectful burial. The time had come to raise in its place a different kind of national government altogether.

Such was Madison's position in 1786. He had come to it slowly and painfully, and only after watching the failure of attempt after attempt to strengthen the Confederation. He himself had taken part in many of these attempts, had started some of them.

His state and Maryland were quarreling again when, in 1783, he ended his first term in Congress and went home, to be elected a few months later to the House of Delegates, the lower house of the Virginia legislature. This time the quarrel between the unneighborly neighbors was not over western lands. That issue had been settled. Indeed, the day was near when the weak Confederation Congress would hand down probably the single most important law ever passed by any Congress—the Northwest Ordinance, the law which divided the West into territories and decreed that as each territory reached a certain size it could enter the Union as a full-fledged state.

The problem between Maryland and Virginia in 1785

was that bogey of the Critical Period—trade between the states. The Old Dominion and 'M——that froward hussy" both used the river that lay between them, the Potomac, for commercial purposes. And day after day they fussed with one another over who had what rights on its grandly rolling waters.

Since Maryland ruled all the river, how should the two states divide up the taxes imposed on foreign goods brought up the Potomac for delivery to people in both states? Under what conditions could a Maryland ship use a Virginia port and vice versa? How much should each state pay toward the maintenance of the lighthouses and buoys? Questions, questions, questions, with different answers to every one of them coming from the two sides.

Stop feuding and get together, said Madison. Let each state appoint a set of commissioners. Let the commissioners meet somewhere and draft an agreement under which the two states could ply the river in peace.

Madison knew that if he proposed this idea from his seat in the legislature in Richmond, Virginia, Maryland would reject it at once as coming from the inner circles of "a foreign government." So Madison slipped the idea to his friend Thomas Jefferson, still sitting in Congress. Jefferson slipped it to Thomas Stone, a delegate from Maryland. Then Jefferson and Stone together slipped it to their governors, pointing out that it was just a little notion that had happened to pop into both their heads at the same time.

The governors endorsed the notion and ordered the arrangements to be made. Alexandria, Virginia, was selected as the place. A time was set. But at the last minute Governor Patrick Henry of Virginia forgot a couple of things. First, he forgot to notify some of the commissioners that they had been appointed. Then, he forgot to tell those commissioners he had notified where and when the meeting was to take place.

Whether Governor Henry really forgot or forgot on purpose would be argued later. Before the war Henry was one of the first men in his state to say, "I am an American first and a Virginian second." Since the war he had become a

Virginian first again. First, last, and all the time. Henry looked with suspicion on any move likely to result in another effort—there had been several such efforts in the past—to give the Confederation the authority to regulate trade among the states. Henry thought the central government already had all the authority it should have. Perhaps more. When the pinch came, he would be in the forefront of Antifederalist opposition to the constitution framed at Philadelphia. When the Maryland commissioners reached Alexandria, they saw no sign of their Virginia counterparts, for the simple reason that the Virginians didn't know they were supposed to be there. So great were the hazards of travel in those days that nobody was expected to get anywhere on time. So the Marylanders waited, only to conclude after a few days that they had been stood up. Whereupon they went home in a snit.

At this moment George Washington came to the rescue of the swiftly vanishing trade pact. Informed of what had happened, he sent messages to all of the commissioners. He urged them to try again and invited them to use Mount Vernon as the site of their talks. There a satisfactory agreement over use of the Potomac was arranged.

The success of the Mount Vernon talks moved Madison to dream a bigger dream. Would it not be a good idea to persuade all the states to send commissioners to a meeting for the purpose of finding remedies for all the country's commercial ills? Some good was almost certain to come of such a convention. Perhaps the commissioners to it, having studied the country's many commercial problems, would go home and urge their delegates in Congress to support an amendment to the Articles giving Congress the power to regulate trade among the states. At the very least, the report issued by the meeting would dramatize the need for a national government equipped with such power.

Two qualities seldom found together in one man lived side by side in James Madison. One was sticktoitiveness. Once Madison decided a thing should be done he never gave up trying to get it done. The other quality was modesty. When he got a good idea, his only interest was in seeing it put into effect. He didn't care who got the credit for it.

Madison knew it would never do for him to suggest the meeting he had in mind. He was a marked man in the eyes of the largely Antifederalist members of the Virginia legislature. They regarded his views on central government as "extreme." If he suggested what was to become the Annapolis Convention, many of them would suspect a dark plot to enlarge the national government at the expense of the states and vote no.

So Madison got his fellow legislator John Tyler (father-to-be of the President of that name) to make the necessary motion. Tyler was known to lean toward strong central government, but his views on the matter were not considered as extreme as Madison's.

Tyler saw to it that the motion was passed. Then he and Madison saw to it that messages went from the Virginian legislature to all the states. Each of them was asked to send commissioners to a convention, to be held in Annapolis for the purpose of considering "how far a uniform system in their commercial regulations may be necessary to their common interest and . . . permanent harmony."

As one of Virginia's commissioners, Madison waited impatiently for the opening of the convention on September 4. But disappointment greeted him in Annapolis. Most of the states had expressed an interest in the convention, but only five had sent commissioners. Fortunately for the future of the union, most of the twelve men who did attend were of the same mind as to what the country needed.

Small, chipper, and almost handsome with his stabbing blue eyes and soft expressive mouth, Alexander Hamilton of New York had long ago suggested that the country create a real national government. To Hamilton's mind the Confederation did not deserve to be called a government at all. Why honor with the name "government" a body that couldn't govern?

George Read of Delaware was of the opinion that the excessive power given to the legislatures of the states had made tyrants of their governments. He looked forward to the creation of a national government strong enough to "swallow all of them up." John Dickinson, recently moved from Pennsylvania to Delaware, was as much a Federalist as ever. Tench Coxe of Pennsylvania couldn't wait to see the nation put up and the states put down.

For several days the twelve nation-minded men waited, hoping more commissioners would arrive. When it became clear no more were coming, they had to admit that the Annapolis Convention was a failure. Or was it?

Obviously they could not suggest "a uniform system" of regulations that would end the endless trade wars between the states. Delegates from five states could not speak for thirteen states.

Just as obviously, there was one thing they could do. They could issue a report suggesting that another convention—a second convention—be called. By way of attracting delegates from all the states, they could see to it that the second convention was not called by just one of the states, as this one had been. This time they would ask the United States, in Congress assembled, to issue the call.

There is reason to believe that Abraham Clark of New Jersey suggested this procedure. There is also reason to believe Hamilton put him up to it. At any rate, Hamilton wrote the report, the "address," as it was called.

Madison stood at his elbow. It is good that he did. For Madison was as tactful as Hamilton was blunt. Hamilton was not a man to curb his tongue or the nib of his quill pen. Left to himself, Hamilton would have written that the Confederation was a mess, and that it should be sent packing and replaced by a real government. Madison agreed heartily, but he pointed out that such frankness would scare off most of the states. Hamilton understood. He watered down his flaming sentences. He suggested "with the utmost deference" that all of the states name commissioners to meet at Philadelphia on the second Monday of the coming May. Once, there, they would not limit themselves to talking about trade problems. The would also "devise such further provisions as shall appear to them necessary to render the constitution of the federal government adequate to the exigencies of the Union.''

The last act of the members of the Annapolis Convention was to have fourteen copies made of Hamilton's address. They sent one to each of the states, one to Congress. This done, they went home, their heads full of questions.

Would the states agree to send delegates to the proposed convention in Philadelphia? Would the Congress give the convention its blessing?

Even as they left Annapolis, the answers to those questions were taking shape in the rolling pastures and dark woodlots of western Massachusetts.

With a salvo of angry shouts and a crackle of musketry, Shays's Rebellion was underway.

Only a few things are known about Daniel Shays, leader of the uprising that carries his name.

He was a veteran of the Revolutionary War with the rank of captain. He learned how to handle a gun at such places as Lexington and Bunker Hill, Ticonderoga and Saratoga. After the war he farmed a patch of land near Pelham, Massachusetts. He was a quiet man, ''not much given to speakin','' according to a neighbor. And he was about thirty-nine when he joined the rebellion, for the same reason many other farmers were joining it—because heavy taxes and mounting debts were driving them mad.

The annual tax on an average-size farm in Massachusetts—two hundred dollars—was more than the owner and his family could hope to earn in the best of years with the best of harvests. Interest on the farmer's mortgage—the money he borrowed to buy his land in the first place—ranged from 25 to 40 percent. If a creditor sued him for past-due payments on a loan, the farmer could look forward to ruin.

Doing business in the Bay State was expensive. A suite brought to collect twenty dollars meant that the farmer would get a bill for thirty-five dollars in legal fees in addition to the twenty he owed. If he couldn't pay, he lost everything—his homestead, his tools, his furniture, "the last potato in his cellar and the only cow or pig in his barn." First the officials of the court sold everything he owned for a fifth of its value. Then they clapped him in jail for the crime of having fallen into debt. In one Massachusetts county the number of men behind bars for debt came to twenty times the number there for all other offenses combined.

The rebellion began as a series of protest meetings in scattered sections of Massachusetts. At Worcester and elsewhere desperate farmers gathered to draw up petitions.

They wanted help from the General Court, the legislature of Massachusetts, in Boston. They wanted lower taxes. They wanted laws that would give them more time to pay their creditors. Living in areas empty of gold and silver, they wanted the state to issue paper money and let them pay both taxes and debts with that. Convinced that all lawyers were "savage beasts of prey," they even asked the legislature to make it a criminal offense to practice law!

Off to Boston went their requests, to be turned down by a legislature controlled by the well-to-do merchants and shippers of the seacoast towns, the so-called men of property to whom the tillers of the soil were indebted.

Goodbye to the widely held belief that the Bay State, home of the town meeting, was a stronghold of democracy. Only aristocrats living hundreds of miles from Massachusetts believed that. John Adams knew better. Town meeting or no town meeting, Adams once observed, his state, like New York, was ruled by "no more than a dozen" large and prosperous families. Certainly the legislature in the summer of 1786 was in no hurry to help its hard-pressed farmers.

So the farmers helped themselves.

No creditor could force a man to pay (or take his property if he didn't) until a court issued orders permitting the creditor to do so. The answer to their problems, the farmers decided, was simple: stop the courts from meeting.

When the time came for the opening of the fall term of the Court of Common Pleas at Northampton on the Connecticut River, the arriving judges found fifteen hundred farmers, armed with muskets and pitchforks, waiting for them on the courthouse lawn.

The judges turned their horses around and galloped home.

At the little market town of Springfield, thirty miles downriver, the local militia made it possible for the Superior Court to open its fall session there. But once inside the building, the judges of the court found themselves sitting in the eye of a storm. Milling in the streets outside, hundreds of angry farmers waved loaded guns and shouted threats. After a few days the judges gave up and went home, leaving most of their work unfinished.

All fall and into the winter these scenes would be repeated. Soon almost no courts of any kind were meeting in western Massachusetts. Soon large sections of the area had become military encampments, with the farmers-turned-soldiers marching and executing the manual of arms under experienced drill masters like Captain Shays. Soon roving bands of rebels and detachments of Massachusetts militia were shooting at each other in the pinewoods.

As most members of both groups were veterans of the war, the few uniforms in evidence on either side were the buff and blue of the Continental Army. To distinguish themselves the two groups wore decorations in their hats. Sprigs of hemlock identified the rebels, strips of white paper the militiamen. Noncombatants forced to travel through the region made a point of carrying both.

To Springfield in Mid-September came Major General Henry Knox, onetime Boston bookseller, Washington's artillery chief during the war, and now Superintendent (Secretary) of War for the Confederation.

Knox was deeply worried. The growing turmoil in his home state put all of his 280 pounds to quivering. It confirmed what he had been preaching for years—that there was no hope for the republic so long as its parts (the states) amounted to everything and its head (the national government) amounted to nothing. "The state systems," he would soon be telling a close friend, "are the accursed things which will prevent our being a nation . . . Smite them in the name of God and the people.''

Concern over federal property had brought the war secretary north from his office in New York City. Back in 1777 Congress had taken a ninety-nine-year lease on ten acres of Springfield land as a site for what was now the Federal Arsenal. Originally the arsenal consisted of a cluster of wooden buildings—storehouses, barracks, repair ships, a foundry for the casting of brass fieldpieces. Now it boasted, in addition, a stout brick magazine, its fortress-like ramparts crowning the low hill overlooking the eastern banks of the Connecticut River. As Knox well knew, the arsenal sheltered 450 tons of military stores. Among them were 1,300 barrels of gunpowder, 7,000 muskets, much shot and shell, and a number of small cannons.

Already there were rumors that, once the rebels got themselves organized, they intended to storm the arsenal and seize its contents. Somehow that catastrophe must be prevented.

At Springfield Knox conferred with Major General William Shepard, commanding officer of the Massachusetts militia in the county where Springfield stood. Shepard had received orders from the governor of Massachusetts, James Bowdoin, authorizing him not only to call up his militia but to enlist additional members for it. Even with this added manpower, his forces would not be big enough to repel a large rebel attack, and both he and Knox realized that posting a few extra men at the arsenal might do more harm than good. A small increase in the guard might act on the rebels like a red flag on a bull. It might prompt them to attack at once, instead of waiting until they were organized.

Knox wrote the governor, pointing out that since the Federal Arsenal stood on the soil of Massachusetts, it was up to Massachusetts to protect it. The governor wrote back that since the arsenal belonged to Congress, Congress should protect it.

Knox hastened back to New York to ask the Congress

to raise a federal army large enough to protect the arsenal. His request put the delegates in a stew.

The entire army of the United States consisted of only seven hundred men. Most of them were stationed at great distances from Massachusetts. None could be spared from his present post.

Still another problem made the delegates hesitate. Never before had they been called upon to send federal troops into a "sovereign state." When it came right down to scratch, the authorities of Massachusetts might consider that action an invasion of their rights. The other sovereign states might take the same attitude. General Knox offered a way around the problem. There was talk in Massachusetts, he said, of "possible Indian troubles" in the western counties. Surely the leaders of the Bay State would not object to the presence of a federal army raised to protect its inhabitants from "savages."

That had a good sound to the delegates. They adopted a resolution authorizing the Secretary of War to bring the United States army up to 2,500 soldiers by recruiting 1,340 men. The resolution suggested that most of them be recruited in New England so as to be in a position to defend that region against "possible Indian attack." Even the delegates from Massachusetts voted for the resolution, although none of them had seen an Indian in their state for a quarter of a century.

Knox's pleasure at the resolution was short-lived. Most of his additional federal force was doomed to exist only on paper. Troops must be paid, and even the enterprising Secretary of War could not pull wages for 1,340 men out of an empty treasury.

The disappointed secretary soon found that about all he could do was fume and write letters. To his onetime commander-in-chief went an especially alarming report.

"Between 12,000 to 15,000 men," he wrote Washington, "are in arms" in western Massachusetts. As for the reasons the farmers gave for rebelling—"high taxes and unjust courts"—those, said Knox, were "as remote from truth as light from darkness." The farmers' real aim was to divide up all the property of the state among themselves. Were their uprising to succeed, all debts would be abolished, all contracts would become worthless pieces of paper.

Knox's fears caught on. From one end of the country to the other, "men of property" trembled. Many who had once hated the very thought of a strong central government changed their minds. Southern plantation owners frowned over reports from the North. "Rebellion" was a scary word to these owners of many slaves. Gathering in their plantation homes to discuss the crisis, they avoided the phrase "Shays's Rebellion." Or they said it in low tones, lest the blacks who plowed their fields and kept their houses get dangerous ideas.

Antifederalists, men whose dread of strong central government would never leave them, began to admit that "something" must be done about the Confederation. Some Federalists were openly gleeful. "The convulsion in New England," said a Philadelphian, would awaken people to the necessity of "energetic" national government. "I beleave," wrote a merchant in Massachusetts, "that the tumults here . . . will alarm the other States and by that Means Congress will Soon have Suffict Powers For the Benefit of the whole."

Small wonder many Americans began to suspect that the Federalist were behind the rebellion. Perhaps they had pricked the farmers to it, knowing that "a resort to anarchy" would convince people of the need for stronger national rule. No proof of this suspicion would ever appear, but in Antifederalist circles the belief that Shays's Rebellion was a Federalist plot would endure for years to come.

While Knox wrote letters in New York, Governor Bowdoin acted in Boston. He summoned the General Court, the legislature, into special session. "Reform!" was the slogan of the hour. Rapidly the legislators passed a spate of laws aimed at making it easier for a farmer to satisfy the tax collector and stave off the bill collector. Some of the new laws were just what the farmers had requested.

But it took time for news of them to penetrate the western counties. By the time it got there, soldiering had become a way of life to the rebelling farmers. And a well-paid way at that.

For suddenly there was money in rural Massachusetts. Hard money! Three shiny shillings a day for every drilling rebel. A fortune to men who hadn't enjoyed the jingle of gold and silver in their pockets for as long as most of them could remember.

Where did the money come from? The state authorities were never able to identify the givers of it. They did learn that the bright coins were being carried from camp to camp and handed out to the rebels by six Massachusetts doctors. They also learned that all the doctors were "notorious Tories!"

Once this knowledge came to hand, the state authorities knew what to suspect. Back-country Massachusetts had more than its share of Tories. These men and women lived for what they called the "counter-revolution," the day when King George would send new ships and new armies across the sea and recover his onetime American empire. Obviously the pro-British elements of New England were fishing in the troubled waters of rural discontent.

At Boston, candles burned late in governmental offices as Governor Bowdoin and his advisers pondered ways and means of suppressing the insurrection. Reform had failed. Force was the only course left open. But force cost money. How could the state raise an army big enough to crush the revolt without raising taxes? High taxes had moved the poor to rebel. Higher ones might move the rich to do the same.

Again General Knox came up with an idea: "Since Congress cannot afford to hire soldiers," he wrote the influential Boston merchant Stephen Higginson, "exertions must be made and something hazarded by the Rich."

Higginson lost no time in recommending this procedure to Bowdoin, and the governor at once saw in the suggestion a way of raising the army he needed without raising taxes. He summoned to his office the Bay State's best-known military figure, Major General Benjamin Lincoln, one of the heroes of the Revolutionary War.

We have no record of their conversation, but we can imagine how it went.

"General Lincoln," said the governor, "I hereby authorize you to raise an army for the purpose of ending the present disorders. You will see to it the courts are permitted to open in the west and that the contents of the Federal Arsenal at Springfield remain where they are."

"I accept the duty, your excellency," said the general. "Just one question if I may?"

"And what is that?"

"How is the army to be paid?"

"I suggest, sir, that you put that question to your wealthy friends."

General Lincoln knew just how to put it to them. He obtained leave to address an exclusive Boston club, made up of rich merchants and shipowners. "Gentlemen," he said, "you know the dangers posed by the insurrection in the west. I suggest that unless you give up part of your wealth now, you will lose all of it later."

Within twenty-four hours Lincoln had raised almost twenty thousand dollars and on January 4, 1787, he moved west at the head of 4,400 state troops. His main destination was Springfield, a hundred miles to the southwest.

The fierce New England winter had come. Blinding snowstorms made the going slow. Hit-and-run attacks by bands of rebels slowed it further. General Lincoln's big army would not get to Springfield in time to deal with the assault on the Federal Arsenal when, in the last week of January, that long-expected event finally occurred.

At Springfield in late January, General Shepard and five hundred Hampden County militiamen were guarding the Federal Arsenal on its low hill above the Connecticut River. Daily reconnoitering the nearby countryside, Shepard's scouts were coming in with disturbing news. Three rebel units were already encamped in the vicinity: four hundred men under Captain Luke Day at West Springfield, just across the river; another four hundred under Captain Eli

Parsons at Chicopee, a few miles to the north on the eastern or arsenal side of the Connecticut; twelve hundred under Captain Shays at Wilbraham, also on the eastern side and even closer to the arsenal.

Shepard's spies were unable to learn when the rebels intended to attack. Nor did Shepard know what sort of progress General Lincoln was making in his march from Boston. He could only hope that Lincoln and his large army would reach Springfield before Shays and his followers decided to move.

Weeks before, Shepard had written General Knox in New York asking authority to use some of the fieldpieces stored in the arsenal. Only Congress could grant that permission and Shepard's request reached that body during one of its long periods of absenteeism. So few delegates were on the floor that all the Congress could do was meet in the morning and vote to adjourn to the next day.

Now, realizing that his little force was outnumbered by the surrounding rebels, Shepard boldly moved on his own, realizing as he did so that he could be drummed out of the service for acting without orders. Obtaining the key entrusted to the guard, he opened one of the arsenal buildings, removed some of the small cannons, and emplanted them in front of the magazine. Their stubby snouts pointed down the long, snow-covered slope up which the attackers would have to come.

If they came. The Hampden County militia commander could only wait and worry.

He need not have worried so much. For in the three rebel camps, fear, indecision, frostbite—and drunkenness—were rampant.

Struggling to keep warm in twenty-five-degree-below temperatures, Luke Day's men at West Springfield were consuming too much rum to be a threat to anyone but themselves.

Imprisoned by man-high snowdrifts at Chicopee, Eli Parsons had given up trying to communicate with the other Shaysite leaders after several futile attempts to do so. Before the month ended, Parsons and his men would be on their way to the warmth of their farmhouse firesides.

At Wilbraham Daniel Shays was already in the midst of the hardest kind of battle a human being can be called on to wage—a battle with the doubts flooding through his mind.

Shays had joined the insurrection in good faith, convinced only armed action could move the legislature in Boston to deal justly with the poor farmers of Massachusetts. Subsequently much had changed. Months before, Governor Bowdoin had issued a proclamation saying that no punishment would be meted out to any rebel who laid down his arms before the end of 1786. Now Shays was beginning to wish that he and his followers had taken advantage of that offer before it faded with the coming of the new year. The legislature had already granted some of the farmers' demands. Had the Shaysites given up the rebellion last year, they could be fighting now for further reforms through legal and peaceful political channels.

Brooding at Wilbraham in that freezing January of 1787, Daniel Shays would like to have walked away from the rebellion that had taken his name. But he knew that he dared not. To run now would be to endanger both himself and the other leaders of the uprising. In the eyes of the state authorities he and they were "traitors," "dangerous radicals."

He knew, too, that Lincoln and a large state army were coming west. He must attack the arsenal before Lincoln arrived or give up the attempt. But before leaving Wilbraham, Shays made one last effort to avoid the bloodshed certain to occur if he marched to Springfield.

He sent a message to General Shepard. It was a plea for amnesty, a request that Shepard see to it that no punishment be handed out to any rebels who agreed to down their arms at once.

Shepard was a genial, kindhearted man. He would have done everything in his power to carry out Shays's request had it reached him. But it didn't. The rebel soldier selected to carry it across the lines somehow lost it in the snow.

Receiving no reply to his demand for amnesty, Shays assumed the answer was no. He sent another message. This one went to Luke Day at West Springfield. Shays wrote that he and his men would be in Springfield on the twenty-fifth. He ordered Day to bring his troops across the frozen river that morning. They would join forces at the foot of the hill leading up to the arsenal.

Luke Day groaned when this instruction reached him. His drunken men would be in no condition to fight on the twenty-fifth. It would be impossible for him to lead them across the river until the twenty-sixth.

He scribbled a note to this effect and gave it to one of his men to carry to Shays. Shays never saw it. Luke Day's message got no farther than the arsenal, its carrier having been seized en route by General Shepard's soldiers. When on the morning of the twenty-fifth Captain Shays and his twelve hundred men marched into Springfield, no troops from across the river were there to assist them.

General Shepard posted himself on the steps of the brick magazine at the crown of the hill. He stationed his soldiers on the grounds, to either side of the steps. In front of them stood the little cannons, manned and primed.

Two hopes tumbled over one another in the general's mind. He hoped that Daniel Shays, on discovering that his allies had not come across the river, would have the good sense to back off. Or if Shays did march to the foot of the hill, the general hoped the sight of the fieldpieces at the top would compel the rebel leader to retreat.

Neither of the general's wishes was granted. From the porch Shepard watched, frowning, as Shays's men spread out at the bottom of the long hill, their thin, ragged lines like moving pencil marks against the whiteness of last night's snow. The general waited until his trained eye told him the Shaysites were within range of his fieldpieces. His first command was that of an American who had no desire to hurt other Americans. He called for a warning shot.

"Shoot over their heads!" he ordered.

The blast was thunderous, the echoes seeming for a time to grow even louder as they bounced down the valley.

Peering into the dense smoke, Shepard thought he saw a slight pulling back on the part of the invaders. But then the smoke parted and he realized that he was wrong.

Shays and his men were still coming up the hill.

"Damn the fools!" the general was heard to exclaim.

His next order was in earnest. "Shoot straight ahead," he commanded.

That did it. Four Shaysites fell to the ground, three dead, the other mortally wounded. Within minutes the rest of them were in flight.

Thus did the spirit of Shays's Rebellion die on the slopes leading up to the Federal Arsenal on that cold January morning. Not that the rebellion itself ended there. Arriving at Springfield two days later, General Lincoln and his Army pursued the fleeing Shaysites.

During the coming weeks there would be skirmishes here and there, some in Massachusetts, some in adjoining states. Shays himself would take refuge in another state, but several of his fellow leaders would be caught, tried, sentenced to death—and then pardoned. In the end, all the rebels, Shays included, would be forgiven. And in the spring of 1787 Shays's Rebellion would be over.

But not forgotten. In their bumbling way the poor farmers of Massachusetts had helped set the stage for the Federal Convention.

9

The Road to Philadelphia

SHAYS'S REBELLION, LET IT BE REMEMBERED, WAS JUST beginning when, in late September 1786, the Annapolis Convention ended with Alexander Hamilton drafting an address calling on the Congress to summon all the states to another convention to be held in Philadelphia.

Congress was slow to act on this recommendation. No less than three requests for such a convention had been presented to the national legislature in the past. Each time the congressmen said no, prodded by the fear that men gathered for the purpose of strengthening the central government would strengthen it too much.

Hamilton's address reached the meeting hall of the Congress in New York on September 20. No cheers greeted its arrival. The delegates voted to refer it to a three-man committee. Reporting a few days later, the members of this group said the matter was too large for them to handle. They suggested it be turned over to a committee to be composed of one delegate from each of the thirteen states.

A motion to do that was seconded and voted. But the thirteen-man committee was never appointed. In the fall of 1786 the Confederation Congress was loath to approve a convention that many people were saying would destroy the Confederation Congress itself.

While the congressmen hemmed and hawed, the states acted. By the end of the year seven of them had endorsed Hamilton's address and elected delegates to the proposed Philadelphia gathering. Under these circumstances the Congress, always the creature of the states, had to act. Hamilton had suggested that the delegates to the convention be authorized "to devise whatever provisions shall appear to them necessary to render the constitution of the federal government adequate to the exigencies of the Union."

The congressmen were not willing to go that far. They had no intention of letting the members of the convention make whatever changes in the government they happened to want. In their official call, issued on February 21, 1787, they instructed the states to send delegates to Philadelphia "for the sole and express purpose of revising the Articles of Confederation."

Each state could select as many delegates as it wished. Virginia chose seven, Madison among them. Washington's name headed the list, but for weeks the general hesitated. Many things urged him not to go. Not the least of them was his memory of the words he himself had spoken in Annapolis on the occasion of his resignation as commander-in-chief of the Continental Army. He had said then that he was retiring from public life "forever." If he went to Philadelphia as a delegate to the Federal Convention, would not people say that he had gone back on his own word?

But over and against that memory came another. How many times, in public, had he complained that the Confederation was too weak and in need of drastic alterations. If now he did not go to Philadelphia, people might decide he had changed his mind. They might take his absence as a sign that he wished the Confederation to remain as it was.

In the end—in March—the general agreed to serve.

* * *

Madison was a busy man during those anxious months before the convention began. He dispatched an urgent request to Paris, where his old friend Thomas Jefferson was acting as America's minister to France. He asked Jefferson to find for him "a few books" dealing with the history and problems of republican government.

Jefferson did not send a "few books." He sent hundreds. "A literary cargo," Madison called them, and as the books poured in, he began reading, taking notes, and thinking.

At his plantation home, between meetings of the state legislature, he spent all the daylight hours in his study. In Richmond, attending sessions of the legislature, he hurried to his quarters in the evening to bend over the "literary cargo."

His research confirmed something experience had long since led him to suspect. A republic is one of the hardest of all governments to keep alive. It tends to be torn apart by the conflict between, on the one hand, the will of the majority and, on the other, the "unalienable rights" of all its citizens to "life, liberty and the pursuit of happiness."

As Madison would say later, the main job of the delegates assembled in Philadelphia would be to find "a republican remedy for the diseases most incident to republican government." They must write into the national constitution what students of political science called "checks and balances." The majority of a national legislature could make bad laws as well as good laws. The country's constitution, therefore, must give the government ways of discouraging the creation of unjust laws or of striking them down even though the majority of the legislators wanted them.

Madison's reading also helped him find the answer to another question long on his mind. How was the national government to get the money to run the country and pay off the war debt?

Early in the decade Madison had assumed that since under the Articles of Confederation the Congress could ask the states for money, it could also force them to pay. Not so, he now realized. One sovereign government could compel another sovereign government to do something only by going to war against it. Short of waging war, Congress could no more force the sovereign states of America to do something than it could force the sovereign states of Europe—England, for example—to do something. There was only one way around this problem: let the national government ignore state lines and operated directly on the people. Instead of giving it the power to ask money from the states, give it the power to tax the people living within them.

Early in 1787 the Virginia legislature sent Madison to New York to begin his second term in the Confederation Congress. Many of the books Jefferson had shipped across the sea went with him. When a few months later he left New York, en route to Philadelphia, he knew exactly what kind of government he was going to fight for at the Federal Convention.

By late spring the newspapers of the country were teeming with articles about the forthcoming meeting. Some spoke of it as the "Fœderal Convention." Some called it "the Grand Convention of the States."

As the opening day neared—Monday, May 14—a certain eagerness welled up over the country, a feeling that a dark night was ending, a day beginning. Recent events had left their mark on people's minds. The quarrel over the Jay-Gardoqui treaty negotiations, the bold action of a few determined Federalists at Annapolis, Shays's Rebellion—these turmoils had won many converts to the cause of strong central government.

No one knew what would happen at the convention. But all thoughtful Americans knew that whatever did happen would have a lasting effect on them and their children.

A Boston newspaper put into words their mingled hopes and fears.

"The Grand Convention of the States," said the *Independent Chronicle,* "will settle forever the fate of republican government."

PART TWO

THE FEDERAL CONVENTION

10

The Place and the People

THROUGHOUT THE SUMMER OF 1787 THE PEOPLE OF Philadelphia talked endlessly of two things: the weather and the Federal Convention.

The weather was brutal. Old-timers pronounced the summer the hottest and wettest since 1750. People had trouble breathing. "At each inhaling of air," a visitor from France wrote home, "one worries about the next one. The slightest movement is painful." Once in a while came a few hours of relief, of cool and drying breezes. More often the relief took the form of soaking rains that left the steaming city steamier than before. Dr. Benjamin Rush, coming and going from the homes of his many patients, likened existence in the Quaker City that summer to "living under Niagara Falls."

Slender, handsome Dr. Rush was not a delegate to the convention. That did not prevent him from talking about it. Neither did it stop his fellow townsmen, although none of them knew what the convention was doing.

A sentry stood at the closed door of its meeting hall. Its proceedings were secret. When Jefferson, still in Paris heard about the rule of secrecy, he was unhappy. Government by the people, he wrote Madison, should always be carried on in full view of the people.

Madison disagreed. He would say later that had the people been allowed to listen in on the convention their criticism would have discouraged the delegates from doing anything at all.

After all, they were not getting together to govern the country, but to find a government for it. They must feel free to think out loud, as it were, to say one thing today and something different tomorrow, without being denounced as "inconsistent" by a watching public. Only by trial and error and with much changing of the mind could they accomplish what their states had sent them to Philadelphia to do. As historian Carl Van Doren has written, the job of the members of the Federal Convention was "to find the best form of government they could agree on" and then let their fellow citizens decide whether they wanted it or not. It was Van Doren's impression that at least some of "the delegates thought of themselves as engaged in a process like that of a creative artist, who insists on finishing his work before he exhibits it. . ."

One state, Rhode Island, refused to send delegates. Of the seventy-four men named by the other twelve states, nineteen never got to the convention. Today we speak of the fifty-five who did get there as the Founding Fathers— a misleading term, as it suggests a parcel of old men. As a matter of fact, seven of them were not yet thirty-two. Only six were over sixty and the average age was forty-three. Benjamin Franklin was the oldest at eighty-one, Jonathan Dayton of New Jersey the youngest at twenty-six.

Madison had once objected to the low quality of the men being sent to the Confederation Congress. He could not so complain of those coming to the Federal Convention. Thirty-four were successful lawyers. Thirty-seven had served in the Congress. All had been active for years in the politics of their home states.

They met in the east chamber of the first floor of the Pennsylvania State House, except for a few weeks in July when noisy crowds, attending a session of the Pennsylvania Supreme Court across the hall, drove them upstairs. It was in their main meeting hall on the first floor that the Declaration of Independence had been signed. Delegates who had attended sessions in this handsome chamber—already popularly known as "Independence Room"—were struck by how little the years had changed it: the same low railing across the back, the same round tables covered with green baize, the same deeply carved panel behind the chair and desk of the presiding officer, the same high windows to either side, their slatted wooden blinds pulled tight shut during most of that sweltering summer of 1787.

But if Independence Room had changed little, the city around it had changed much. In recent years Philadelphia had become larger and noisier. One of the early acts of the Founding Fathers was to persuade the city authorities to layer Chestnut Street with gravel. The gravel deadened the clop-clop of passing horses and the rattle of carriages and drays.

Today we know much of what went on that summer behind the closed and guarded door of Independence Room. Although stiff and colorless, the official record penned by the secretary, Major William Jackson, outlines the proceedings. Nine personal records kept by members of the convention fill in the details.

These many records take us into convention hall. They let us hear the voices of arguing men, sometimes quiet and reasonable, other times quivering with rage or heavy with despair. They show us how more than once the convention came within a hair of collapsing. How for four months, for five to seven hours a day, the delegates labored. How almost down to the closing hour they wondered what if anything they could accomplish. How after they adjourned and went home, it was to wonder for an even longer period whether the American people would accept what they had accomplished.

Of the nine personal records the fullest and most revealing by far is the one kept by Madison. During the convention the Virginian was on his feet, taking part in the debate, 161 times. How, one wonders, did he manage to be so active and still keep so complete a record?

It nearly killed him, he confessed later. "I chose a seat in front of the presiding member," he explained, "with other members on my right and left . . . In this favorable position for hearing all that passed, I noted in terms legible and in abbreviations . . . intelligible to myself, what was read from the Chair or spoken by the members . . . I was not absent a single day, nor more than a casual fraction of any hour in any day. . ."

Far shorter than Madison's personal notes, but highly useful, were the ones kept by William Pierce of Georgia.

Forty-seven-year-old Pierce had fought in the war as an artillery officer. Subsequently he had prospered as a merchant in Savannah, and in 1787 he was a member of both the Congress and the Federal Convention. Like Madison he came to Philadelphia from New York, but whereas Madison came early and remained to the end, Pierce came late and remained only a few weeks.

During his short stay his eyes and ears were alert. In Madison's personal record of the Federal Convention we hear the delegates; in Pierce's account we see them. The Georgian had a sharp eye for those outward features and traits that suggest so much about the inner person.

Pierce found two of his fellow delegates endlessly diverting: New York-born Gouverneur Morris of the Pennsylvania delegation (no relation to Robert Morris) and Roger Sherman of Connecticut. Pierce considered Gouverneur Morris the most brilliant member of the convention. Certainly he was the most talkative. He made more speeches—173—than any other delegate. Sometimes he angered his listeners. Sometimes he shocked them. But he never bored them.

No man was fonder of the good things of this earth. Morris loved fast horses, glittering social affairs, and pretty women. A carriage accident had deprived him of his left leg. He stomped about now on a wooden peg, assisted by a thick cane.

For all his love of worldly pleasures, he was no fop. He was tall and heavy-set—the other delegates called him "the big boy"—with an unusual amount of face, glowing eyes, and a deep, throbbing voice.

Pierce considered Roger Sherman of Connecticut "the oddest shaped character I ever remembered to have met with," adding that the "oddity of his address, the vulgarisms that accompany his public speaking . . . make everything that is connected with him gross and laughable." But Pierce admitted that when the rough-hewn, square-faced Yankee got up to talk he made every bit as much sense as did the elegant Gouverneur Morris.

Fascinating to Pierce were the similar attitudes voiced by these two outwardly unlike men. Born at Morrisania, one of the largest of New York's huge estates, Morris was an aristocrat and made no bones about it. "No society can endure without an aristocracy," he announced. A rural shopkeeper and lawyer and the son of a poor shoemaker, Sherman did not believe the common people from whom he sprang had the knowledge needed to run a government and was never reluctant to say so.

Still, when it came down to scratch, both men readily put aside their conservative prejudices in what they considered to be the interest of the country as a whole. Like his friend Hamilton, Gouverneur Morris believed that a wide distribution of power was the secret of good government. Give all the power to the rich, he said, and they will oppress the poor. Give all to the poor and they will oppress the rich. Give an equal amount of power to both groups and they will check and control each other. Roger Sherman took a similar view. He offered no objections to putting into the Constitution clauses favorable to the common people, just so long as they were balanced by clauses equally favorable to the "uncommon people."

What most stands out about these remarkable men is their freedom from hypocrisy. On the floor of the convention Morris and Sherman said what they thought. Neither indulged in the practice, common to politicians, of giving democracy more lip service than support, of saying kind things about the poor while actually working for the rich.

Such honesty of speech seems to have been fairly widespread among the members of the Federal Convention.

One would have to search far to discover two more outspoken men than James Wilson of Pennsylvania and George Mason of Virginia. William Pierce would have been on solid ground had he given those two the same high marks for brilliance he gave Gouverneur Morris. Like James Madison, the thoughtful and swift-speaking Mason and the dry-speaking and dry-looking Wilson brought to the convention a deep understanding of the strengths, weaknesses, and problems of government by the people.

Not that they had the same things to say there. A native of Scotland and appropriately dour in manner, Wilson was an ardent Federalist. Some of the most eloquent arguments for "consolidated government"—meaning strong central government—would come from his lips during the course of the convention.

On the other hand, white-haired, spirited George Mason was an ardent Antifederalist. The sixty-two-year-old master of Gunston Hall plantation admitted that the Confederation needed strengthening. But as the convention got underway, indignation sprang from his very pores as it dawned on him that most of his fellow delegates were bent on replacing the Confederation with a consolidated national government.

In the end Mason would refuse to sign the Constitution. He would charge that it favored the "commercial interests" of the mercantile-shipbuilding North at the expense of the "landed interests" of the rice- and tobacco-growing South.

Mason was not the only prominent Antifederalist to be named to the Federal Convention. Willie Jones of North Carolina and Patrick Henry of Virginia were also elected, but both refused to serve. Both suspected the convention would move in the direction of consolidated government.

"I smell a rat" was how Patrick Henry put it when he decided not to attend.

In later years Antifederalist Richard Henry Lee would say that, had Jones and Henry attended the convention, they and a few others might have turned the tide. He could not make the same complaint about Mason. Mason accepted the challenge. At Philadelphia he put himself on the firing line, endlessly battling for his Antifederalist beliefs. Among the delegates who fought with him were Luther Martin of Maryland, Robert Yates and John Lansing, Jr., of New York, and Elbridge Gerry of Massachusetts. But Martin, Yates, and Lansing would leave Philadelphia in a huff before the convention was over. Only Mason and Gerry would stick it out to the end.

As was true of all gatherings in that era of difficult travel, the convention did not begin on time.

The members drifted slowly into Philadelphia. The convention would be half over before some of them got there. Most came from distant homes. A few, like Madison and Pierce, came down from New York City, temporarily abandoning their seats in Congress to participate in the convention.

Madison was the first to arrive, reaching the Quaker City on May 3, "eleven days early," his biographer writes, "for a convention that would begin eleven days late." For ten days he was the only delegate on hand other than the eight Pennsylvanians, all residents of the city.

Madison put the time to good use. He continued his study of the problems of republic government. He called on Dr. Benjamin Franklin.

No one of consequence came to Philadelphia without calling on the doctor. And no one came away from Franklin's comfortable house at the rear of a flower-bright courtyard off Market Street without feeling the fuller and the merrier for it.

In the opinion of his fellow citizens—indeed, in the opinion of the world—the doctor was the second man in America, second only to George Washington. Everyone knew

Franklin's story: how migrating to the Quaker City in his seventeenth year, a poor boy from Boston, he became within little more than a decade its leading citizen: owner-editor of its most popular newspaper and prime mover in the many civic improvements that made eighteenth-century Philadelphia one of the most civilized cities on earth.

The world of letters knew him as the founder, or one of the founders, of Philadelphia's first circulating library, of the American Philosophical Society, of what is now the University of Pennsylvania.

The world of science knew him as the man who, by putting a kite into the sky, discovered what many had long suspected but could not prove, that lightning is electricity. In 1782 he presented to a geologist-friend in France an amazingly accurate description of a startling scientific idea that would not be accepted until almost two hundred years later—the theory of plate tectonics, which explains how the surface of the globe has taken form and the causes of volcanoes and earthquakes.

The world of diplomacy knew him as the chief negotiator of the treaty that ended the Revolutionary War, as the spokesman for American interests in the courts of the Old World for thirty years in all.

Returning to Philadelphia in 1785, after his long stay abroad, Franklin reluctantly but cheerfully accepted the office of president (governor) of Pennsylvania. The years had exacted their price. He suffered now from gout and from what his doctors called "the stone." His ills made walking difficult, riding in a carriage impossible. Going the one-eighth mile between his home and the State House, he traveled in a sedan chair, borne by four husky prisoners from the Walnut Street jail.

At home, finding hot water a comfort, he spent much of his time in a huge copper bathtub. Here he did his reading, his book perched on a movable attachment he himself had invented. Those visiting him in his house or under the spreading mulberry tree in his courtyard saw, as one of them wrote, "a short, fat, trunched old man in a plain Quaker dress, bald pate and short white locks."

The years had neither staled his mind not bridled his humor. When the founders of a college named in his honor suggested he repay the compliment by giving them a bell, he sent them instead a trunkful of books. "What an institution of learning needs," he told them, "is not sound but sense."

From May 13 on, Madison was no longer the only out-of-town delegate in Philadelphia. On the afternoon of that hot, bright Sunday the other Virginians began coming into town.

Chiming bells and military ceremonies marked the arrival of Washington. The general had reserved quarters where Madison was staying, at the home of Mrs. Mary House at Fifth and Market Streets. But Washington's old friend, Robert Morris, one of Pennsylvania's delegates to the convention, would not hear of his staying there. "Warmly and kindly pressed by Mr. and Mrs. Morris to lodge with them," Washington noted in his diary, he accepted and had his luggage removed to their three-story brick house on Market Street near Sixth.

From here, on clear days, he would walk the one block to the State House, wearing a blue coat and a cocked hat, with his hair dressed in a queue and "crossed and powdered." Crowds gathered to watch him pass. In the eyes of most Americans the stately Virginian was a figure larger and more perfect than life. Few noticed how often a look of pain crossed his features, provoked by the ill-fitting false teeth a French doctor had made for him at Newburgh. One observer, a young man from New Jersey, did notice that the general "walked along . . . and seemed pressed down in thought."

On the official opening day of the convention—Monday, May 14—such delegates as were in town gathered at ten in the morning in Independence Room.

It was understood from the beginning, and would later be written into the rules, that no business would be conducted unless seven states had quorums on the floor. It was also understood that on all motions placed before the convention, each state could cast one vote and that the votes of a majority of the states present would be enough to pass or reject any resolution. If a majority of the members of a quorum approved a motion, the vote of that states registered as "aye." If they disapproved, as "no." If there was an even number of them on hand and half voted aye and half voted no, the vote of the state registered as "divided," meaning that it cast no vote at all. As to when a state had a quorum, that depended on the instructions issued by its legislature. Four of Pennsylvania's eight delegates constituted a quorum. Three of Virginia's seven could cast the vote of that state.

Because on may 14 only two states, Virginia and Pennsylvania, had quorums, no record was kept of the official opening session. The delegates remained together about an hour, talking with one another and getting acquainted. Only one decision was reached—to do no business until seven quorums were on hand. Meanwhile, whatever delegates were in town were to report to the State House at ten o'clock each morning.

Thus matters stood for a week and a half. Madison made the most of the wait. As his fellow Virginians arrived, he brought them together at the Indian Queen, a coffeehouse and inn on Fourth Street between Market and Chestnut. There, each afternoon, they exchanged views. There, little by little, they put on paper their idea of the kind of government the country ought to have—a series of propositions soon to be known as the Virginia Plan.

It was during this period of marking time that Washington delivered the only speech he is known to have made at the Federal Convention. The general had seen the failure of too many efforts to improve the national government to be optimistic about this one. "It is too probable," he said, "that no plan we propose will be adopted." Even so, he hoped the delegates would not be guided by what they thought the people of the country wanted. He urged them to trust their own minds and consciences. "If to please the people," he said, "we offer what we ourselves disapprove, how can we afterwards defend our work? Let us raise a standard to which the wise and honest can repair.''

At last, on the morning of Friday, May 25, enough quorums were on hand for the delegates to close the door of their meeting hall and declare the convention in session.

Official act number one was to elect a chairman, a presiding officer. This was a mere formality. For that post every man in the room had the same person in mind. The plan had been for Franklin to nominate Washington, but a steady and droning rain had kept the ailing philosopher at home. Robert Morris did the honors for him, and Washington, unanimously elected, took the chair.

The convention then took other necessary steps. It framed the rules under which it would proceed. This took a few days. It named William Jackson to be the secretary for the body. Having taken his place on the platform, Major Jackson collected the credentials—the documents showing the right of the delegates to be there, along with the instructions given them by their state legislatures.

Thus began a governmental gathering unlike any ever attempted before. it was Charles Pinckney of South Carolina who one morning expressed in words two of the most noticeable characteristics of the Federal Convention: the abiding fear of its members that the American people might not approve of their work and the uniqueness of what they were trying to do.

''Our government,'' the bright and chipper South Carolinian said that morning, ''must be suitable to the people, and we are perhaps the only people in the world who ever had sense enough to appoint delegates to establish a general government.''

11

The Virginia Plan versus the New Jersey Plan

BUT NOW THAT THE DELEGATES HAD COME TOGETHER, what sort of general government would they try to establish?

Would they bow to the demand by Congress that they meet for the sole and express purpose of revising the Articles of Confederation? Or would they draft what an angry Antifederalist later called "a frame of government as different from the Articles as Hell is different from Heaven"?

Would they revise or would they create?

When shortly after noon, Tuesday, May 29, the delegates finally turned to the business that had brought them together, that question was on every mind.

Edmund Randolph began the proceedings by reading and explaining the Virginia Plan, the series of propositions or resolutions that he and his fellow Virginians had formulated during their conferences at the Indian Queen coffee shop and inn.

Tall and uncommonly handsome, with richly molded features and expressive eyes, Edmund Randolph had crammed a lot of activity into his thirty-three years: aide-de-camp to Washington during the opening months of the war, member of the convention called to write his state's first constitution, attorney-general of Virginia for two terms, member of Congress for two terms, now governor of his state and leader of its delegation to the Federal Convention.

It is interesting that Randolph should have introduced a plan so many parts of which would find their way into what is now the United States Constitution. He himself was not sure that the country needed the strong government that the plan outlined. He had come to Philadelphia believing that a few changes in the Articles of Confederation would take care of matters. Reluctantly he had gone along with the ideas agreed to at the Indian Queen. Perhaps Madison worked on him. In his quiet way Madison could be persuasive.

The Virginia governor began his speech by listing some of the things he thought a general government should be able to do. It should be able to protect the country against foreign foes. It should be able to provide benefits, such as more and better roads and canals, that the individual states could not develop on their own. It should be able to regulate trade between the states. It should be strong enough to quiet quarrels between the states and to suppress "seditions," such as Shays's Rebellion, when they erupted within them.

The present government could not do these things. The weakness of the Confederation, Randolph declared, had encouraged the states to make "incroachments" upon it. He mentioned the frequency with which the states had taken unto themselves powers that only the general government was supposed to exercise. Only the Congress was entitled to make treaties, but Virginia had made a separate treaty of peace with England. Congress alone had the right to raise a navy, but nine states had navies of their own.

Four of the men who listened to Randolph that Tuesday afternoon had helped frame the Articles of Confederation.

One of them was Elbridge Gerry of Massachusetts. Gerry was a merchant and shipowner. He was a scrawny little man with a long, thin nose that he thrust now this way and now that, like an accusing finger, when he got up to speak. Politically he was given to blowing hot and cold on big issues. On balance, however, his sentiments were those of an Antifederalist. His face wore a worried look. When he was excited, which was most of the time, he squinched his eyes and stuttered.

The other signers of the Articles in Randolph's audience were the two Morrises, Gouverneur and Robert, and John Dickinson, who had come to this gathering as the leader of the Delaware delegation.

Randolph did not want to offend the four men who had signed the Articles. He made a point of noting that the defects of the Articles could not be blamed on those who made them back in 1777. At that time, he said, the country was in "the infancy of the science of constitutions." No one could foresee then the troubles of the critical period. Now the time had come for Americans to learn from their mistakes and improve their general government accordingly.

Having made these and other points, Randolph read the Virginia Plan to the delegates in his fine and vibrant voice.

Filled with ideas Madison had been recommending for months, the plan suggested the creation of a national government to consist of three divisions: an executive, to be headed by one or more presidents; a judiciary, to consist of what are now the Supreme Court and the lesser federal or district courts; and a two-house legislature, to consist of what during the ensuing debate would be spoken of as "the first branch" (the House of Representatives) and the "second branch" (the Senate).

Several of the resolutions of the Virginia Plan suggested how the members of the three divisions of the government should be elected or appointed. Others listed the powers each division should be allowed to exercise—powers far more extensive than those exercised by the Confederation.

When Randolph finished, the light was fading at the tall

windows. There was no time for a discussion of the Virginia Plan that day. In the few minutes left before adjournment two delegates, Charles Pinckney and Alexander Hamilton, asked permission of the presiding officer to take the floor.

Pinckney requested that a plan he himself had written be sent to Major Jackson's desk. To the desk it went, to be lost in the shuffle and never debated.

Alexander Hamilton made what seems to have been his first remarks at the Federal Convention. Poor Hamilton! His voice would be heard occasionally in the days to come, but his vote would never count.

The governor of New York, George Clinton, was a militant supporter of state sovereignty. So were most of the members of the New York legislature. Hamilton's fellow delegates—Robert Yates and John Lansing—were Antifederalists. On every issue coming before the convention, their votes for weak government would render Hamilton's vote for strong government of no moment. Even when Hamilton was the only New Yorker on the floor, he could do nothing. Under the instructions issued by the legislature of New York, two of its three delegates had to be there to cast the vote of that state.

When Hamilton rose it was to point out that the members of the convention faced an important decision. They could leave things as they were. In that case America would continue to be nothing more than "a league of states" and never become a true nation. Or they could scrap the Confederation, replace it with a "consolidated government," and become a nation.

Hamilton's voice was thin, but the earnestness with which he spoke compelled the others to heed him. Already full-blown in that brilliant mind was a vision of the kind of country he wanted his America to be. In later years his vision would clash with the different vision held by Thomas Jefferson. Jefferson looked forward to a happy America. Hamilton wanted a great and powerful America.

Standing at the New York table that Tuesday afternoon—a slight but impressive figure—the thirty-two-year-old lawyer from New York expressed the hope that the Founding Fathers would invent a government under which the American people could achieve the high destiny he wanted them to have.

After he sat down, the delegates agreed to begin their discussion of the Virginia Plan on the following morning.

For almost three weeks the delegates discussed the Virginia Plan in an informal manner.

Many votes were cast. None was considered official because throughout this period the delegates met in what is known as the Committee of the Whole.

Suggestions placed before the Federal Convention were handled exactly as the Congress and the state legislatures handled such things. The process began with a vote to refer the proposal to a committee. The committee decided what should be done about the matter and reported its recommendation to "the House," meaning to the full membership meeting in its regular manner. Only the vote taken in the House was official.

For a proposal as important and complicated as the Virginia Plan, a different process was followed. Instead of being referred to a committee composed of some of the members, the Virginia Plan was referred to a committee composed of all the members.

This was the Committee of the Whole.

Invented centuries before by the British Parliament, the Committee of the Whole turned out to be a useful method for men come together to change a government. Every man realized that the votes taken in committee were only for the purpose of determining "the sense of the body." Every man knew that when the committee rose and the members again met as the House—in regular session, that is—he would have another chance to vote on every issue. He could then change his vote if meanwhile he had changed his mind.

Most important of all, ticklish issues—those on which agreement could not be reached in committee—could be put off in the hopes that by the time the official vote came up in the House agreement could be reached.

More often than not, agreement on ticklish matters was reached at the Federal Convention only after a great deal of what eighteenth-century American politicians called "out-of-doors work." The phrase "out-of-doors" went back to the early meeting of the Continental Congress, when the delegates found that the only way they could settle big arguments was to talk about them in small groups off the floor. Many of these informal conferences took place in the State House yard. Hence the practice of speaking of agreements arrived at behind the scenes as out-of-doors work.

Whenever the Federal Convention went into Committee of the Whole, Washington left the chair and sat at the Virginia table. Another member, elected by the delegates—Nathaniel Gorham of Massachusetts—occupied his place until the committee voted to meet again as the House. At that point Washington returned to the chair.

Shortly after ten o'clock Wednesday, then, Washington left the chair, Gorham took over the presiding officers duties, and the members formed themselves into a committee to debate the Virginia Plan.

Again Edmund Randolph got things started. Overnight he and other delegates had done some out-of-doors work. Randolph wanted to withdraw the opening resolution of the Virginia Plan, which he considered "too general," and replace it with certain "more specific" statements.

The original opening resolution, as read to the delegates the day before, said "the articles of Confederation ought to be so corrected . . . as to accomplish the objects proposed by their institution; namely, common defence, security of liberty and general welfare."

Gouverneur Morris, Randolph revealed, had argued that it was "absurd" to open the Virginia Plan with a call to revise the Articles of Confederation when all of the other resolutions of the plan called for the creation of a different kind of constitution.

Randolph thought Morris's objections to the opening resolution well grounded. He, therefore, wished to propose in its place a resolution stating "that an Union of the States, merely fœderal, will not accomplish the objects proposed by the articles . . . namely 'common defence, security of liberty, and general welfare.' "

Silence—strained and prolonged—greeted Randolph's words. The bewilderment on many faces revealed what every man in the room understood. Already, with the proceedings barely underway, the convention had reached a moment of decision.

Many seconds passed before Charles Cotesworth Pinckney of South Carolina broke the silence.

Eleven years older than his cousin Charles Pinckney, Charles Cotesworth was even more the elegant gentleman. Educated at Oxford University in England and trained for the bar in London, he practiced law in the mother country for a while before going on the "grand tour" of Europe. Coming back to his own country, he fought with the patriot armies and was captured when the British overran Charleston, the capital of his state.

During his captivity the British officers tried hard to win him over to their side. They assumed that because Charles Cotesworth Pinckney spoke and acted like an Englishman he thought like one. In truth, he was as republican in his sentiments as George Mason of Virginia. Even in an age when political orators went in for grand language and rhetorical flourishes, the speeches of Charles Cotesworth Pinckney stood out. "If I had a vein," he once declaimed, "which did not beat with the love of my country, I myself would open it. If I had a drop of blood that could flow dishonourably, I myself would let it out."

He meant every flaming word of it. And when he rose to comment of the newly proposed opening resolution of the Virginia Plan, he meant what he had to say about that, too.

Did Governor Randolph realize what he was asking the members of the convention to do? He was asking them to approve a resolution stating that no amount of fixing could make the Articles adequate to the needs of the country. But the United States, in Congress assembled had sent them to

Philadelphia "for the sole and express purpose" of making the Articles adequate. If they voted for a resolution saying that couldn't be done, then there was only one legal and honorable procedure for them to follow: they must adjourn for keeps, pack their bags, and go home!

Charles Cotesworth Pinckney's remarks loosed an avalanche of talk by the other delegates.

Gouverneur Morris said that the new opening resolution raised questions in his mind, even though he himself had suggested it. The resolution said that a "merely fœderal" government, meaning the Confederation, could not run the country properly. In another of its resolutions the Virginia Plan suggested the establishment of a "supreme . . . national" government. But under the Confederation the state governments were supreme. How could a supreme national government be established unless at the same time the supreme state governments were abolished? For the life of him, Morris couldn't see how one country could have two supreme governments.

No problem there at all, said John Dickinson. He called Morris's attention to the solar system. The main body of that system was the Sun. Its satellites—Earth and the other planets—revolved around it. The Sun was supreme over all, but each of the planets was supreme within its own orbit.

Dickinson saw no reason why the general government and the states couldn't function in the same way. Let the national government, he said, be "supreme" over matters of interest to the country as a whole. Let each state be "supreme" over matters of interest to that state alone.

It remained for James Wilson to go to the heart of the problem. He felt that the delegates were wasting time arguing over the meaning of terms. In Wilson's opinion it didn't matter whether you called the general government "Fœderal," "national," "supreme," or "consolidated." What mattered was how you set it up. To be effective, he said, the general government must not be compelled to operate on the states as the Confederation had to do. It must be empowered to operate directly on the people.

James Madison was quick to voice his approval of this view, having long ago come to the same conclusion.

Randolph, in his tactful way, ended the argument over the meaning of "fœderal," "national," and "supreme." Noting that these terms puzzles some of the delegates, he suggested that consideration of the new opening resolution of the Virginia Plan be postponed to some later date. Time would prove this maneuver a good one. The argument over terms would never come up again.

The suggestion put by Randolph having been agreed to, he moved that the delegates consider one of the other Virginia resolves—the one saying that the general government ought to have three "supreme" divisions: an executive, a legislature, and a judiciary.

Now the delegates were back on familiar ground. Several of the states already had three-part governments, and these were working well. After a brief and quiet debate, Randolph's motion "passed in the affirmative." Of the eight fully represented states on the floor, six voted for a three-part national government: Massachusetts, Pennsylvania, Delaware, Virginia and the two Carolinas. Only Connecticut voted no. New York, with two of its delegates present, divided. To no one's surprise, Federalist Hamilton voted aye and Antifederalist Yates voted no.

Rapidly the delegates moved on to other sections of the Virginia Plan. Several resolutions won almost instant approval. But the more important ones—those dealing with the legislature and the executive—gave birth to quarrels that would extend far into the summer and on one occassion threaten to send the Founding Fathers home with nothing to show for their pains.

So intense was the argument over the makeup of the legislature and how its members should be elected that from the beginning everyone saw that here were problems difficult to handle. Even after votes were taken to determine the sense of the body, everybody knew that when the Committee of the Whole rose and reported its recommendations to the House, these problems would have to be thrashed out all over again.

Much of the debate over the executive had to do with whether that department should be headed by one or more individuals. Many delegates balked at the idea of having a single president. They said it smacked of royalty. It took their minds back to their sufferings under a powerful one-man executive called King George III.

To these delegates the thought of giving all the might of the executive department to one person was frightening. What if a person named to the presidency turned out to be a bad man? What if he were incompetent? What if he had poor judgment and surrounded himself with evil or incompetent advisers?

Settling these matters would take time. Only after sixty votes and hours of talk would the delegates agree to put all the powers of the executive department into the hands of one person.

By what method should the president be elected?

Into the effort to settle that question, too, went many votes and much talk.

None of the delegates thought the people of the country should choose their chief executive directly. Direct election by the people, some of them believed, would subject every presidential election to interference by "foreign powers." The United States, during its early years, was more open to the influence of Europe than would be the case later. Never mind the three thousand miles of ocean between the New World and the Old. Adjoining the new republic on the north was Canada, owned and governed by Great Britain. To the south and west, Spain still controlled vast sections of what is now the United States. It was common knowledge that Britain, Spain, and other European nations would like to have a say in the affairs of the new American republic. Were the people allowed to vote directly for their chief executive, how easy it would be for some European nation to trick them into putting into the presidency a man secretly in the pay of a foreign power.

Another objection to direct election was that it might split the country into many political factions, each battling for a different candidate. This situation would almost certainly give rise to turbulence and disorder.

No, said the delegates, direct election of the president would not do. Another way must be found.

One suggestion was that the national legislature choose the president. This idea was at once objected to on the grounds that a president so chosen would have no independence. He would be the creature of the legislative department.

It was James Wilson who suggested that the actual voting for the president be done by a small group of electors. Wilson believed, as did other delegates, that a small body of men would be in a better position than the people as a whole to examine the abilities and character of the various presidential candidates and choose the right one.

Wilson's idea caught on quickly, but it raised another argument. How should the electors be chosen? Some delegates thought the state governors ought to select them. Others wanted the people to do so.

On and on the debate ran. The convention would be almost over before the delegates agreed on a method for selecting the president. Into the Constitution would go a clause authorizing the creation of an electoral college. Each state would name a certain number of electors to this body, and each state would be allowed to decide how its electors were chosen.

The delegates had discussed every word of the Virginia Plan when, on the morning of June 14, William Paterson of New Jersey sprang a surprise on them.

Forty-two-year-old, Irish-born Paterson was a wisp of a man, only five feet two. His face was bland as an apple and he had the inward-looking eyes of a thinker. Getting to his feet, he told Chairman Gorham that before the Committee of the Whole rose he would like to place before the delegates another set of resolutions, to be known as the New Jersey Plan.

* * *

As revised by the Committee of the Whole the Virginia Plan opened thus:

"RESOLVED, That it is the opinion of this Committee, that a national government be established, consisting of a Supreme Legislative, Judiciary, and Executive."

As offered by Paterson on Friday, June 14, the New Jersey Plan opened:

"RESOLVED, That the articles of Confederation ought to be so revised, corrected and enlarged, as to render the federal Constitution adequate to the exigencies of Government, and the preservation of the Union."

The Virginia Plan called for the creation of a new government. The New Jersey Plan called for a revision of the old government.

For three days the delegates, still meeting as a committee, debated the New Jersey Plan.

It was a great moment for the Antifederalists. Yates and Lansing of New York could not lavish enough praise on the New Jersey Plan or enough scorn on the Virginia Plan. By diminishing the state governments, they argued, the Virginia Plan would diminish the liberties of the people. By keeping the state governments strong, the New Jersey Plan would keep those liberties.

To date, Alexander Hamilton had said little on the floor of the convention. But that feisty Federalist could not sit silent while this hymn of praise for state sovereignty fell from the lips of his fellow New Yorkers.

Suddenly Hamilton was on his feet. Once up he stayed there for almost six hours. He did not damn the New Jersey Plan. Neither did he praise the Virginia Plan. Hamilton thought the country should have a far stronger, a far more "high-toned" government than even the Virginia Plan proposed. Not caring for either plan, he suggested one of his own. Hamilton regarded the government of Great Britain as the finest in the world. He would like to see the Americans imitate it, but he was aware that they could not copy it exactly. To begin with, they hated the thought of a king. A sad state of affairs, he sighed, but not a hopeless one. Hamilton saw no reason why the Americans couldn't enjoy the stability and order that he thought only a king could provide by putting at the head of their government a president elected for life.

In Hamilton's eyes England's House of Lords was a "noble institution." Tied to the interests of the nation by their large properties, he said, the members of the second branch of the British Parliament could be counted on to curb whatever rash and dangerous changes the first branch, the House of Commons, chanced to propose.

Could the Americans create a House of Lords? Of course not, said Hamilton. They wanted no peerage, no titled class. No dukes or earls for them. Even so, he pointed out, they could discourage rash and dangerous changes by the first branch of their legislature (the House of Representatives) by letter the persons elected to the second branch (the Senate) stay in office for life, like the president.

Perhaps some of the delegates frowned at Hamilton's remarks. Perhaps not. Most of them, especially the older delegates, listened indulgently to this fascinating young man from New York. They knew that once he had got his monarchial ideas off his chest, they could simply ignore them and go on with their business.

That's what happened. No attempt was made to debate the "Hamilton Plan" and a few days later its author left Philadelphia to stay for a while in New York—saddened at the failure of the Founding Fathers to take his advice, but comforted by the knowledge that he had done all one man could to save the republic from what he later spoke of as the "poison" of democracy.

On the afternoon of Tuesday, June 19, the Committee of the Whole rose. When the delegates came back together on the morrow, they would do so as the House, sitting in their regular manner, with Washington in the chair.

In their last important vote that day they agreed to submit a revised version of the Virginia Plan to the House. This action had the effect of rejecting the New Jersey Plan.

Now all of the delegates knew the path the convention was going to follow. The Founding Fathers were not going to try to patch up the Articles of Confederation, as suggested by the New Jersey Plan. They were going to try to write a new constitution along the lines outlined in the Virginia Plan.

All of them also knew that it was going to take a lot of work to unravel the snarls already come to light. In the near offing lay the great crisis of the Federal Convention—the battle between the little states and the large states.

12

Little States versus Large States

THE BATTLE BETWEEN THE LITTLE STATES AND THE large states grew out of the arguments over the makeup of the national legislature and how its members should be selected.

Under the Articles of Confederation each state could cast one vote in the Congress. This meant that the smallest state, Delaware, had as much power there as the largest state, Virginia, even though the population of Virginia was at least fourteen times greater than that of Delaware.

The makers of the Virginia Plan thought this arrangement unfair. In their opinion the states with larger populations deserved to have more power in Congress than those with smaller ones. The Virginia Plan, therefore, suggested that how much power each state exercised in the national legislature be determined by "proportional representation." Under this system how many persons a state could send to Congress would depend on how many people lived within its borders.*

The delegates were just beginning their first long session as a Committee of the Whole when, in late May, they were asked to consider the proposal that the makeup of the legislature be based on proportional representation. At once spokesmen for some of the smaller states were on their feet complaining. Give the bulk of the power in Congress to the large states, they said, and soon the little states would find that they had nothing to say about running the country. Nothing whatsoever.

Votes were taken to discover the sense of the body. These ballots showed that a majority of the states favored proportional representation.

So what! said five of the states. So what, said Delaware, New Jersey, Connecticut, New York, and Maryland. The convention could vote for proportional representation as many times as it wished. Those states would never accept it.

It is worth noting that some of the opponents of proportional representation were not small states. New York was the fifth largest state in the Union. It sided with the small states because New York's Antifederalist delegates, Yates and Lansing, wanted to see the Confederation continued. Maryland was the sixth largest, but most of the time it sided with the small states because its most influential delegate, Luther Martin, was an Antifederalist.

It is also worth noting that not all the proponents of proportional representation were large states. Georgia was the third smallest. But Georgia's location put it in a different category from Delaware, New Jersey, and Connecticut.

---

* The original Virginia Plan suggested that the number of representatives and senators allowed each state to be based either on the size of its population or on the amount of its wealth. But the use of wealth as a basis was never well thought of and in time was dropped from consideration. In the end, the main argument over proportional representation came down to this question: should each state continue to exercise equal power in the Congress as in the past, or should the number of persons it could send to Congress and the number of votes it could cast there be proportioned to its population?

It was a Southern state, dependent for its livelihood, like the rest of that region, on slave-worked rice, indigo and tobacco plantations. On proportional representation and other important issues Georgia voted with its Southern neighbors, the Carolinas and Virginia, all large or medium-large states.

When the argument over proportional representation broke out in late May, slight and aristocratic George Read of Delaware began the speeches for his and the other small states. Read was one of the hardest-working men on the floor of the convention and a born worrier. Large pouches sagged under his stern eyes. The eyes themselves were those of a man who slept too little. Read pointed to the instruction issued by the legislature of his state. Those orders forbade him and the other five Delaware delegates to support any change in the voting rules of the national legislature. On that issue their hands were tied.

If the larger states wanted to establish a union on the basis of proportional representation, said Read, let them do so. Delaware would never join it. Nodding heads at other tables indicated that neither would New Jersey, Connecticut, New York, and Maryland.

On June 11 Roger Sherman jumped into the little-state versus large-state argument. Record-keeping William Pierce of Georgia gave special heed to the Connecticut Yankee's remarks.

Sherman's New England twang annoyed gentlemanly Pierce, but Sherman's words delighted him. Sherman proposed what he thought might be a way out of the dilemma. Give the large states what they wanted, he suggested, by basing the membership of the House of Representatives on proportional representation. Give the small states what they wanted by letting each state have an equal number of votes in the Senate.

His words provoked a stir in the room, the scrape-scrape of chairs being moved. Many faces brightened. Even some of the delegates from the small states looked happier. From men on both sides of the argument came the statement that

Sherman's suggestion had merit. They promised to think about it.

They were still thinking about it when on Wednesday, June 20, the delegates, meeting again in their regular manner with Washington in the chair, began their consideration of the Virginia Plan as revised in committee.

Once more they went through the plan word by word. Once more they found themselves in agreement on several important points. Then, on the twenty-seventh, the matter of proportional representation arose again and the atmosphere changed. What only yesterday was reasonable debate suddenly became a frenzy of words.

On the twenty-seventh and again and the twenty-eighth, votes were cast. These showed that the larger states did not take kindly to Sherman's compromise. Neither did the smaller states.

Maryland divided on the issue, but the other members of the small-state group—Delaware, New Jersey, Connecticut, and New York—consistently refused to back off from their demand that every state be given the same number of votes in both branches of the national legislature.

Voices were rising, tempers with them, when Benjamin Franklin asked leave to read a speech he had written on a paper that trembled in his old hands.

Franklin was the peacemaker of the convention. A couple of weeks earlier he had tried to quiet a stormy debate by sharing a funny story with the delegates. Now he tried again. He read his speech in a soft, hesitant voice, looking so directly at Washington as he spoke that a stranger coming in would have thought the two long-time friends were having a private chat.

The old man described himself as distressed at the wrangling all around him. After all, the delegates had not come together to fight with one another. They had assembled for the purpose of "consulting in peace on the means of establishing our future national felicity." What they were attempting called for patience and wisdom. In every argument each side must be willing to give as well as take.

"The small progress we have made after 4 or 5 weeks of . . . continual reasonings with each other," said Franklin, ". . . is methinks a melancholy proof of the imperfection of the Human Understanding. We indeed seem to feel our own want of political wisdom, since we have been running about in search of it."

Franklin had a suggestion. All wisdom, he said, came from "the Father of lights." Let the delegates, therefore, arrange to have a chaplain or chaplains—one or more of the local ministers—open each session of the convention with prayers. "I have lived, Sir, a long time," Franklin said, "and the longer I live, the more convincing proofs I see of this truth—*that God governs in the affairs of men.*"

Out of respect for the old man one delegate moved and another seconded a motion calling for the appointment of a chaplain. But, as every delegate knew, the convention had no funds. It could not afford a chaplain. The motion was never voted upon, and on the following day—Friday the twenty-ninth—the warfare between the little states and the large states flared again.

All day Friday and all day Saturday it continued to flare.

Virginia's Madison and Pennsylvania's Wilson did much of the talking for the large states. Both men stressed similar points. A truly national government, both asserted, was one that not only operated directly on the people but also operated in accordance with the wishes of the people. How could the national lawmakers know the wishes of the people unless those states that had the most citizens were allowed to send the most representatives to both branches of the national legislature?

Luther Martin of Maryland and Gunning Bedford, Jr., of Delaware did much of the talking for the smaller states.

In his fortieth year or thereabouts, Martin was a husky man with wide shoulders, a short nose, a grating voice, and a fondness for the bottle that in later years would prove the undoing of his brilliant legal career. His main speech lasted a day and a half. A rambling oration, it stretched the already tightened nerves of his listeners almost to the breaking point.

Bedford was an even larger man, "tall, corpulant and impetuous," according to one of the record-keeping delegates. In one of his speeches on Saturday the forty-year-old attorney-general of Delaware succeeded in doing the impossible. He sent a chill through the stifling heat of the convention's meeting hall.

"I do not, gentlemen, trust you!" he shouted at the delegates from the larger states. Put proportional representation into the Constitution, Bedford warned, and his state would do more than withdraw from the Union; it would protect its interests by seeking an alliance with one of the "foreign powers" of the Old World!

Alarming words to men whose country only recently had won its independence from the most powerful of those foreign powers. Later Bedford apologized for his shocking threat. He called it one of those careless statements that escape a man in the heat of argument. Maybe he meant it. Maybe not. That he said it at all is a measure of the high feeling coursing the meeting room of the Federal Convention on that blistering afternoon.

Two days later, on Monday, July 2, Roger Sherman put into words what many of the delegates were beginning to think. It seemed to Sherman that the convention had come to a "full stop." The states had rejected his compromise and no other had been proposed.

Sherman was sad. He supposed the convention would have to break up now. But perish the thought! He shrank at the prospect of having to tell his friends back in Connecticut that the best minds in America had come together and accomplished nothing.

Surely, he said, something could still be done.

Charles Cotesworth Pinckney responded to Sherman's challenge. Pinckney suggested the appointment of a committee, to consist of one delegate from each of the states. It would be known as the "grand committee" and its task would be "to devise and propose some compromise."

A motion was made, seconded, voted, and the committee was named.

The someone pointed out that the grand committee would need time to do its work. Besides, the Fourth of July was coming up and the delegates ought to be free to attend the ceremonies. The time had come for the convention to enjoy a holiday.

The necessary formalities took a few minutes. Then the delegates adjourned, having decided to hold their next regular meeting on the fifth of July.

13

The Glorious Fourth and the First Compromise

Eighteenth-century Philadelphia was widely and accurately regarded as the "celebrating-est" city in America. Independence Day, 1787, put every bell in town to clanging and every gun to booming. It enlivened the Commons with wheeling soldiers and filled every tavern from the Lilliput on the New Jersey shore of the Delaware River to Gray's Ferry on the Schuylkill River with noisy merrymakers.

At noon Washington and most of the other delegates listened to an oration by one James Campbell at the Reformed Calvinist (Lutheran) Church on Race Street. Campbell saluted the visitors as "Illustrious Senate." "To you," he told them, "your country looks with anxious expectations, on your decisions she rests, convinced that men who cut the cords of foreign legislation are competent to frame a system of government which will embrace all interests, call forth our interests, and establish our credit."

One wonders what Mr. Campbell would have said had

he been aware of the frightening disarray among the members of the Federal Convention.

On the morning of the fifth, the grand committee made its report to the convention.

The members of the committee had discussed a variety of plans, only to decide in the end to come back to something very close to the compromise Roger Sherman had offered. To what Sherman had suggested, the committee added only one provision. Designed to win over the larger states, this additional provision dealt with this question: which of the two branches of the national legislature should be put in control of the purse strings of the nation?

Whereas Roger Sherman's plan consisted of only two major suggestions, the plan the grand committee now placed before the convention consisted of three such suggestions:

1. That in the House of Representatives (as Sherman had urged) each state be allowed one representative for every forty thousand, later changed to thirty thousand, of its inhabitants.

2. That in the second branch of the national legislature (again as Sherman had urged) each state be allowed the same number of senators; and

3. That only the larger and more democratic House of Representatives (this was the added provision) be allowed to frame appropriation bills, meaning laws saying how the public funds were to be spent.

The debate that followed was long and earnest, but on the whole quiet. None of the flashes of ill will, none of the harsh statements and shouted threats that had marked the debate on the eve of the Glorious Fourth. By the end of business on July 13 the battle between the little states and the large states was over, settled by an agreement to base membership in the House on proportional representation, to base membership in the Senate on equal representation, and to let the House—and only the House—originate money bills.

Because the battle between the smaller states and the larger ones came close to breaking up the convention, many historians have described the agreement that settled it as the "great compromise" of the Constitution.

But at least two members of the Federal Convention did not see things that way. Gouverneur Morris saw them otherwise. So did James Madison. Morris spoke of what he considered the most critical fight on the floor of the convention as "the struggle between the two ends of the union." Madison agreed. "The difference of interest in the United States," he said, "lay not between the large and small but between the Northern and Southern states."

In July, when Madison made this remark, the delegates were deep into the argument that would end with the introduction into the Constitution of another compromise.

At the center of this argument lay the problem of slavery.

14

The Slavery Compromise

THE MINUTE THE DELEGATES BEGAN THINKING ABOUT basing membership in the House of Representatives on population* the subject of slavery, then legal in all thirteen states except Massachusetts, whose constitution forbade it,† entered the debate.

Under proportional representation how much power each

---

* In 1787 nobody knew for sure the populations of the states. Probably they were close to the figures yielded by the first national census three years later. At that time, 1790, those figures were: Virginia, including what are now West Virginia and Kentucky, 819,287 (of whom 304,967 were slaves); Massachusetts, including what is now Maine, 477,377 (no slaves); Pennsylvania, 434,373 (3,757 slaves); North Carolina, including what is now Tennessee, 429,442 (102,356 slaves); New York, 340,120 (21,324 slaves); Maryland, 319,728 (103,036 slaves); South Carolina, 249,073 (107,094 slaves); Connecticut, 237,946 (2,764 slaves); New Jersey, 184,139 (11,423 slaves); New Hampshire, 141,885 (158 slaves); Georgia, 82,548 (29,264 slaves); Rhode Island, 68,725 (948 slaves); Delaware, 59,094 (998 slaves).

† The constitution adopted by Massachusetts in 1780 proclaimed all the inhabitants of that commonwealth to be free and equal. Massachusetts, however, was not the first state to ban slavery. That honor belongs to Vermont, which did so in 1777. Although organized as a state in 1777, Vermont was not admitted into the Union, as the fourteenth state, until 1791.

state got in the House would depend on how many persons lived within its borders.

But what about the country's half million slaves? Were slaves persons or were they property? A simple comparison shows why this question quickly became a burning issue at the Federal Convention.

South Carolina's 249,000 inhabitants made it a larger state than Connecticut with 240,000. But a hundred thousand South Carolinians were slaves, whereas Connecticut had less than three thousand slaves. If slaves were counted as persons, larger South Carolina would get the larger number of representatives in the House. If they were not counted as persons, smaller Connecticut would get the larger number of representatives.

Most of the slaves lived in the five Southern states, Maryland, Virginia, the two Carolinas, and Georgia. The people of these states made their living by growing and selling huge crops of tobacco, rice, and indigo. Because the cultivation of these crops required an enormous number of workers, the Southern leaders regarded slavery as vital to their economy.

Relatively few slaves lived north of Maryland. Most of the people in those states made their living from commerce and small farms. They did not need slaves. Indeed, many had long since decided that the keeping of slaves was unprofitable. By 1787 the movement to ban slavery was well advanced in the North. Within a few years slavery would be gone, or going, from most of the Northern states.

To say that slavery was on its way out in the North is not the same as saying that the people of that region contributed nothing to the growth of what Gouverneur Morris, in a speech at the Federal Convention, called the 'nefarious institution" of human bondage.

Morris's attack on slavery was really an attack on the plantation owners of the South. He spoke of the "rich and noble cultivation" in the Northern states. He contrasted it to "the misery and poverty which overspreads the barren wastes of Virginia . . . and other states having slaves."

But in this attack on a great moral wrong Morris chose to overlook the presence in the state of his birth, New York, of twenty-one thousand slaves. Nor did he mention a fact known to every delegate: many wealthy New England shipowners owed their fortunes to profits from the sale to Southerners of slaves brought across the Atlantic on Northern-owned vessels.

What Morris ignored, delegates from the South made much of. As the argument over whether slaves were persons or property waxed warm, they had no qualms about pointing out that Southerners were not the only Americans who had benefited financially from the "nefarious institution." So had many Northerners.

The Federal Convention was not yet three weeks old when the slavery issue arose. On Monday, June 11, four delegates, three of them from the South, proposed what was to become the main part of the slavery compromise.

They suggested that for purposes of determining membership in the House of Representatives each state be allowed to count three-fifths of its slaves as persons.

Elbridge Gerry of Massachusetts sprang to his feet. Sheer horror deepened the already deep worry lines in his pinched face. It was Gerry's understanding that Southerners used their slaves the way Northerners used their farm animals—to till the soil. If the South could count its slaves as persons, said Gerry, then the North should be permitted to count its "horses and oxen" as persons.

Off and on for weeks the argument raged. But from the beginning everybody knew how it was going to end. Unless an endorsement of slavery went into the constitution, at least two states—South Carolina and Georgia—would walk out of the convention. Perhaps all the Southern states would walk out.

Either way there would be no Constitution, no strong central government. And the "nefarious institution" would go right on.

By no means all of the opponents of slavery in the convention were Northerners. Madison pointed to slavery as a supreme example of how "a majority . . . united by a common sentiment" can make life miserable for a minority. "We have seen the mere distinction of colour," the little Virginian said, "made . . . a ground of the most oppressive dominion ever exercised by man over man."

George Mason, always vigorous, was on this subject also angry and sad. "Slavery," he said, "discourages arts and manufactures. The poor despise labor when performed by slaves . . . Slaves produce the most pernicious effect on manners. Every master of slaves if born a petty tyrant."

Mason was not sparing himself. He himself was the master of some two hundred slaves.

"Slaves," he went on, "bring the judgment of heaven on a Country. As nations can not be rewarded or punished in the next world they must in this. By an inevitable chain of causes and effects providence punishes national sins, by national calamities."

But Mason knew—and Madison knew—that mere words could not uproot slavery from those regions whose leaders thought they must have it to support their economy. On the thirteenth of July the delegates did what they had to do to give their country a more efficient general government. Into the Constitution went the main clause of the slavery compromise, the clause that made three-fifths of the slaves persons in the eyes of the census taker.

Other clauses were added later. One of the more important forbade the importation of slaves into the United States after the year 1808. Another authorized the federal government to tax imported slaves, much as it was allowed to tax other kinds of property brought into the country from abroad.

In none of the clauses of the slavery compromise did the words "slave" or "slavery" appear. Their absence suggests that at least some of the Founding Fathers were not happy with a compromise so at odds with the goals for which the Revolutions was fought.

One of "his first wishes," Washington said in a letter to Jefferson, was "to see some plan adopted by which slavery in this country might be abolished by law."

★☆★☆★☆★

15

The Constitution

$\mathbf{A}$FTER THE GREAT COMPROMISES WENT INTO THE CONstitution in mid-July, the convention moved toward its conclusion with the steadiness of a clock. Important questions remained, yes. But answers to them came quickly.

Under the rule of equal representation, how many senators should each state be allowed? This problem stirred a long and at times heated argument, but the final vote—giving two senators to each state—was unanimous.

What about new states, particularly those that in time would be carved out of the vast Western lands? Should they come into the Union with the same rights as the original thirteen states? Or should they come in under special arrangements? The delegates decided to leave this matter to Congress. The years ahead would see the creation of thirty-seven new states. Thanks to rules issued by various congresses, every one of them would begin its life in the Union on equal terms with the others.

What about amendments? No changes could be made in

the Articles of Confederation unless they had the approval of all the states. Antifederalist members of the convention wanted to see this same rule written into the new Constitution. The Federalists did not. Experience, they argued, had shown that all the states could never agree on any amendment. As Madison often pointed out, the new constitution, if accepted by the states, would become "the Supreme Law of the Land." Unless the Supreme Law could be changed as conditions changed, it would soon become a worthless piece of paper. To prevent this, said the Federalists, the approval of three-fourths of the states should be enough to amend the Constitution.

The Federalist won this argument. As finally written, the Constitution would provide two ways for adding amendments. Under one method, two-thirds of the members of both houses of Congress could suggest an amendment, and whenever three-fourths of the states approved the suggestion, it would go into the constitution. Under the other method, the legislations of two-thirds of the states could order Congress to call a convention for the purpose of changing the Supreme Law. Three-fourths of the states having approved of the changes, they would take effect.

Madison would have liked to give Congress the right to veto—his word was "negative"—any state law that the national legislators considered contrary to the letter and spirit of the Constitution. After much discussion the delegates decided against this. They voted instead to list in so many words exactly what powers the Congress would exercise. Prominent among these were the power to levy and collect taxes and the power to regulate commerce among the states.

Under what rules should the Constitution be adopted or rejected?

Much and lively argument showed that this was not one question; it was a tangle of questions. To begin with, the Confederation Congress must give the proposed Constitution its blessing and then ask the states to ratify it.

But who was to do the actual ratifying? On the floor of the convention opinion divided, as it so often did, along Federalist-Antifederalist lines.

The Antifederalists wanted the state legislatures to do it. Years before, the state legislatures had ratified the Articles of Confederation. It was only right and proper that they do the same for the Constitution.

No, no! said the Federalists. The Articles of Confederation had created nothing but a league of states. The Constitution contemplated a true national government, drawing its power directly from the people and operating directly upon them. Let the people decide!

The Federalists won this argument, too. Under the Constitution, as finally written, each state would call a special ratifying convention whose members would be chosen by the voters.

At what point in the ratifying process should the government outlined by the Constitution be considered in effect? The Antifederalists did not want to see it in operation until all thirteen of the states had endorsed the Constitution. The Federalists saw no reason why endorsement by nine of them shouldn't do.

Again the Federalists triumphed.

"The ratification of the Conventions of nine States," the seventh and final article of the Constitution would read, "shall be sufficient for the establishment of this Constitution between the States so ratifying the same."

On the afternoon of Thursday, July 26, the Federal Convention adjourned for ten days, having first created what is called a Committee of Detail. While most of the delegates vacationed, the five members of the committee drafted the first version of the Constitution. For five weeks, beginning August 6, the delegates considered this version. Changes were made, answers found to questions still hanging fire.

Then the delegates created another committee. They called this one the Committee of Style. Its five members drafted a second and more polished version of the Constitution, a version very close to the federal Constitution as we know it today.

On the morning of Wednesday, September 12, the committee presented this almost final version of the Constitution to the convention. Gouverneur Morris had done most of the writing of it, but another member of the committee, William Samuel Johnson of Connecticut, made the report.

Small, quiet-spoken, sixty-year-old Johnson was just beginning his three-year term as president of New York City's Columbia College, now Columbia University. Always addressed as "Dr. Johnson," he was highly respected for his pleasant disposition, his modesty, and his great learning.

He read some portions of the new version of the Constitution. He outlined others. The delegates followed his words on printed copies of the document.

The Committee of Detail had added an opening paragraph, a preamble, to the Constitution. The Committee of Style had revised it somewhat.

"We the People . . ." it began.

As these words rang out, a look of surprise overspread many faces. All the delegates had heard the words before. But now, about to consider the document they had written for the last time, many of them realized for the first time what a strange new thing they had wrought.

As far back as any of them could remember, the makers of America's governments had always thought in terms of the states. Now they were about to put the finishing touches on the framework of a government that would look beyond the states—to the people.

It was an awesome moment. None of them would ever forget it.

"We the People of the United States," Dr. Johnson read, "in order to form a more perfect Union, establish justice, insure domestic tranquility, provide for the common defense, promote the general welfare, and secure the blessings of liberty to ourselves and our posterity, do ordain and establish this Constitution for the United States of America."

When Dr. Johnson finished, the delegates began what was to be a four-day discussion of this almost final version of the Constitution.

Mason of Virginia was not pleased with it. Already the

master of Gunston Hall had announced that if the convention approved the Constitution as written he would "cut of his right hand" rather than sign it.

One of Mason's objections was to that clause in the Constitution under which the Congress could pass laws regulating commerce. Mason pointed out that there were only five Southern states as against eight Northern states. He feared that the commercial regulations voted by a Northern-dominated Congress would always favor the economic interests of the North at the expense of those of the South.

Now Mason offered another objection to the Constitution. It contained no bill of rights.

The earnest Virginia statesman did not have to tell the other delegates what he meant by a bill of rights. Every state constitution contained such a bill. Its various clauses guaranteed freedom of speech and press, freedom of religion, the right to trial by jury for a citizen accused of a crime, and the right of the people to assemble and protest the actions of their government. Mason indicated that if these guarantees of the rights of man were written into the national Constitution, he might change his mind and go along with it.

Roger Sherman took the position that since the state constitutions contained bills of rights, there was no need to put one in the national Constitution. "The State Declarations of rights," said Sherman, "are not repealed by this Constitution; and being in force are sufficient."

Mason shook his head. He noted that the national Constitution would be the Supreme Law of the Land. If Congress saw fit to deprive the people of freedoms guaranteed by the state constitutions, the states would find it hard to do anything about it.

Gerry of Massachusetts agreed with Mason. He moved that a bill of rights be added to the Constitution. Mason seconded the motion.

The official record describes the motion as passing "unanimously in the negative," meaning that is was rejected. Massachusetts did not have a quorum on the floor, but all of the other states voted no.

Time would prove this vote to be the Federal Convention's greatest mistake. In the almost year-long fight over whether the Constitution should be ratified or not, the absence from it of a bill of rights would prove to be the most telling argument against its adoption.

By the end of business on Saturday, September 15, the Constitution was in its final form.

At six o'clock that afternoon Edmund Randolph put the crucial motion—that all the states agree to it as written. All of them did.

Then the convention ordered the Constitution to be engrossed. Under this order an expert penman was hired to make a perfect copy, which the Founding Fathers would be asked to sign. We do not know the name of the penman who on Sunday inscribed the words of the Constitution on four sheets of parchment.

At eleven o'clock Monday morning the tap-tap of Washington's gavel brought the convention to order for the last time.

The day was mercifully cool. Through open windows a breeze played across the handsome east chamber on the first floor of the Pennsylvania State House. Only a week or so before a local newspaper had reported that things were going so well in this meeting room that people were beginning to speak of it as "Unanimity Hall." In truth, there was no unanimity in it. Disagreement, the clash of wills, tension—these qualities had taken over the convention during its opening sessions. They were still there in its closing hours. Documents as useful and durable as the Constitution of the United States are not brought forth in sweetness and light. They are the products of great mental and moral sweat.

Practically every delegate at that last meeting of the Federal Convention was dissatisfied with one or more parts of the Constitution. Several had said as much at length, and the echoes of Washington's gavel still hung in air when Benjamin Franklin asked leave to have his say on the subject.

Again the old man had written his words on a piece of paper. But this time he was too unwell, too unsteady on his gouty legs, to read them himself. His friend and neighbor, James Wilson, read them for him.

"Mr. President," the speech began, "I confess that there are several parts of this constitution which I do not at present approve, but I am not sure I shall never approve them: For having lived long, I have experienced many instances of being obliged by better information or fuller consideration, to change opinions even on important subjects . . . the older I grow, the more apt I am to doubt my own judgment and to pay more respect to the judgment of others. Most men . . . as well as most sects in Religion, think themselves in possession of all truth . . . Steele, a Protestant . . . tell the Pope that the only difference between our Churches in their opinions of . . . their doctrines is that the Church of Rome is infallible and the Church of England is never in the wrong."

Were there smiles on some delegates' faces at this point? Of course there were.

"Though many private persons think almost as highly of their own infallibility as that of their sect," Wilson read on, "few express it so naturally as a certain french lady, who in a dispute with her sister, said 'I don't know how it happens, Sister, but I meet with nobody but myself that's always in the right'—*Il n'y a que moi qui a toujours raison.*' "

Was there laughter in the room at this point? Of course.

"In these sentiments," Franklins's speech went on, ". . . I agree to this Constitution with all its faults . . . because I think a general Government necessary for us, and there is no form of Government but what may be a blessing to the people if well administered, and believe farther that this is likely to be well administered for a course of years, and can only end in Despotism, as other forms have done before it, when the people shall become so corrupted as to need despotic Government, being incapable of any other . . .

"On the whole," the old man's speech ended, ". . . I

can not help expressing a wish that every member of the Convention who may still have objections to [the Constitution] . . . would with me, on this occasion doubt a little of his own infallibility, and to make manifest our unanimity, put his name to this instrument.''

Here Wilson sat down and Franklin himself moved that the Constitution be signed. A second was heard. Then came a brief debate.

Hamilton had not said much in recent weeks. He spoke now. He echoed Franklin's plea that the delegates give at least a show of unanimity by signing the document they had framed.

Born to poverty in the West Indies, the son of an unwed mother, Hamilton knew what it was to grow up in a broken home. He did not want to see his adopted home, America, falling apart; and he was convinced that under the weak Confederation it would do just that. he was not pleased with the Constitution as written. It did not provide the country with anything like the strong central government he thought it should have. But it would be strong enough, he felt, to keep the family of the states together.

Not only did Hamilton intend to sign the Constitution; he also intended to throw all of his great talents into the long, hard fight to persuade the states to ratify it.

The Committee of Style had prepared a letter to be sent to Congress along with a copy of the Constitution. It was a request that Congress lose no time in approving the document and in submitting it to the states for ratification. One delegate rose to offer a strange suggestion. Apparently every man in the room had some doubts about the Constitution as written. That being the case, he suggested that instead of signing the Constitution itself, they simply put their names on the letter to Congress.

No halfway measures, cried Charles Cotesworth Pinckney, leaping to his feet in anger. Faultful human beings, the gentlemanly South Carolinian pointed out, could never produce a perfect constitution. This one was the best they could accomplish. Therefore, let all the delegates sign to show that they stood behind what they had done.

In time the delegates ran out of breath and the ceremony began.

Washington signed first. Then, one by one, the others walked up to the desk of the presiding officer and signed the handsomely engrossed document.

Thirty-nine signatures in all.

But fifty-five men had participated in the convention. What happened to the other sixteen? Most of them failed to sign simply because they were not in Philadelphia at the time of the signing ceremony. But two of them, Robert Yates and John Lansing of New York, had long since served notice that were a constitution written they would not sign it. In the near future a third, Luther Martin of Maryland, would announce that had he had been present for the ceremony he would have given that "engrossed farce . . . an enthusiastic negative."

Of those who were there, three kept their seats, refusing to sign: Mason and Randolph of Virginia, and Gerry of Massachusetts. Within the secrecy of the convention meeting hall all three had voiced the reasons for their refusals. During the next few months the country as a whole would hear what those reasons were.

The ceremony of signing was still underway when Franklin offered his last remarks. No written words this time. No one speaking his words for him. The old man spoke them himself, quietly, sitting in his chair.

All summer Franklin had wondered about the design on the back of the presiding officer's chair. It showed a sun, a reddish-yellow disk with golden rays.

All summer he had asked himself, Is it a setting sun or a rising sun?

Now, said the old man with a twinkle, he had the answer to his question.

It was a rising sun!

On that optimistic note the Federal Convention ended.

That evening the delegates dined together at one of the local inns. Next morning the out-of-towners began leaving Philadelphia.

With them went the satisfaction of having done what their states had sent them to Philadelphia to do. With them, also, went a sense of nagging uncertainty. Would the American people accept what they had done or would they reject it?

Ahead lay the long, harsh debate between the country's Federalists and its Antifederalists. The Federalists were convinced that only by adopting the Constitution exactly as written in Philadelphia could the high aims of the Revolution be realized. The Antifederalist were just as firmly convinced that if the Constitution as written were adopted, those high aims would be lost forever.

PART THREE

THE GREAT DEBATE

16

The War of Words, Ideas, and Blows

Two days after the convention ended, a Philadelphia newspaper, the *Pennsylvania Packet*, published the Constitution in full.

Already other printed copies of it were moving by post road and packet boat to every corner of the country. Soon, from Maine to Georgia, Americans were reading what the Founding Fathers had written. Soon Madison was telling Jefferson that the Constitution absorbs "almost the whole political attention of America." Soon the battle between Federalists and Antifederalists was on. It would rage for months.

Most of the time it was a battle of words and ideas. But not always. There were riots in city streets, brawls in taverns. Challenges to duels were heard. No doubt some duels occurred, with men settling their differences over the Constitution by hacking at one another with swords or shooting at one another with pistols.

As the battle took form, both sides rushed into print.

Richard Henry Lee of Virginia poured his carefully thought-out objections to the Constitution into a widely read pamphlet entitled *Letters of a Federal Farmer*. Governor Clinton of New York poured his into a series of newspaper articles, each of them signed "Cato."

Coming to the defense of the Constitution, Hamilton and John Jay of New York and Madison of Virginia published the scholarly and still much-studied essays now known as *The Federalist Papers*.

Both sides used what Americans two hundred years later would call "dirty tricks."

In Virginia the antifederalists circulated a false report. The report stated that Madison had changed his mind and was about to issue a condemnation of the Constitution.

When it became know that most of the delegates elected to the ratifying convention in New York were Antifederalists, the Federalists began strewing the roads with tree stumps and boulders. They hoped by this action to discourage some of the "Antis" from traveling to Poughkeepsie, where the convention was held.

As the terms of the proposed Constitution became known, the first reaction of more Americans than not was a blend of shock and fear. Shock that delegates sent to Philadelphia to revise the old government had produced instead the blueprint of a new one. Fear that the shift of the country's political power from the states to the nation would produce a general government so distant from the common people that nevermore would they be able to control it.

Quickly many Americans got over their original fears. These people became the supporters of the Constitution, the Federalists. Others did not get over them. They became the opponents of it, the Antis. Generally speaking, Federalism tended to be strongest in the more heavily settled parts of the country along the Atlantic. Antifederalism tended to be strongest in the western counties of the original states and out in the new frontier communities of what are now the states of Kentucky and Tennessee.

* * *

Antifederalist objections to the Constitution took many forms.

"There is no declaration of rights." With these words Mason of Virginia opened a widely read "Address to the People," first published in a Philadelphia newspaper.

Overnight the opening sentence of Mason's article became an Antifederalist slogan: "There is no declaration of rights." On the floor of nearly every state ratifying convention that cry would be heard.

At first the Federalists answered it by repeating the arguments against a bill of rights, first raised on the floor of the Federal Convention, Every state had a bill of rights, Wilson of Pennsylvania reminded a crowd that filled the State House yard in Philadelphia. Since the state bills remained in force, there was no need to put one in the national Constitution.

Later Madison and other Federalist leaders found a different way of handling this pressing issue. They pointed to the ease with which the proposed Constitution could be changed. Adopt it as written, they begged. Get the new government going, and then add a bill of rights to the Constitution by amending it.

Richard Henry Lee of Virginia gave the Antifederalists another point around which they could rally. As the Constitution framed in Philadelphia was faulty, said Lee, let Congress call a second Federal Convention for the purpose of writing a better one.

The Federalists saw in this suggestion a sly effort to delay ratification, perhaps forever. A second Federal Convention would simply produce another imperfect constitution. Then the great fight would have to be fought all over again. Get on with it, the Federalists said in effect. Endorse the Constitution now and improve it later.

To some of the Antis the most alarming part of the Constitution was the next-to-last paragraph of Article I, Section 8.

That paragraph called for the establishment of a capital city for the nation in a "District," known now as the District of Columbia, to be no more than "ten miles square."

No state would own this District. The nation would own it and Congress would rule it.

This seat of the national government, some Antis predicted, would be a "fortified town." They pictured it as largely occupied by a "standing army," ready at any moment to march out and subdue the people. All the wealth of the country would be drawn into this fortified area, leaving the rest of America a vast region of impoverished peasants like Europe.

Some of the more conservative Antis were not worried that the riches of the country would flow into its fortified capital. Their fear was that the country's "deadbeats," those who owned money and wouldn't pay, would flee into the District, thus putting themselves beyond the reach of their state courts—and their creditors. Soon, these Antis said, the national capital would be a community of bankrupts and ne'er-do-wells.

Baptists living in back-country Virginia wanted no part of a Constitution that failed to guarantee freedom of religion. Too long, in the past, had these devout people had to pay taxes to help support an official state religion, the Church of England. Many Protestants looked with horror on the statement in the Constitution that "no religious test shall ever be required as a qualification to any office or public trust under the United States." They shuddered to think what this could mean. Someday a Jew or a Moslem or some other non-Christian might be appointed or elected to high govermental position, possibly even to the presidency itself.

To many Antifederalists the most frightening clauses of the Constitution were those that empowered Congress to tax the people. With no bill of rights to stop them, the Antis argued, the national tax collectors would spread locust-like over the country, invading the privacy of homes, killing men, and raping women.

Yes, many, varied, and, in some cases, nightmarish were the fears of the Antifederalists. But at the center of all of them lay the unshakable belief that the government proposed by the Founding Fathers would not be a democratic one. It would be an aristocracy.

Melancton Smith, one of the Antifederalist leaders in New York, said it. Himself a man of wealth and property, Smith said that if the Constitution were accepted, the new government would "fall into the hands of the few and the great." It would be "a government of oppression."

Amos Singeltary said it, speaking as a delegate to the Massachusetts ratifying convention in Boston. Singeltary was an old farmer from Worcester County. He was a self-educated man. No schoolroom had ever held him, but he had lived through the stirring beginnings of the break with England at Boston and Lexington, Concord, and Bunker Hill.

"Some gentlemen," Singeltary said, "have called on them that were on the stage in the beginning of our troubles, in the year 1775. I was one of them. And I say that if anybody had proposed such a Constitution as this in that day, it would have been thrown away at once. It would not have been looked at . . . Does not this Constitution take away all we have—all our property? Does it not lay all taxes, duties, imposts, and excises? And what more have we to give? . . . These lawyers and men of learning, and moneyed men that talk so finely, and gloss over matters too smoothly, to make up poor illiterate people swallow down the pill, expect to get into Congress themselves. They expect to be the managers of this Constitution, and get all the power and all the money into their own hands. And then they will swallow up us little fellows . . . just as the whale swallowed up Jonah."

Similar thoughts flowed from the talented pen of one of the first women ever to lift her voice in the American political arena. This was Mercy Otis Warren, author of the first history of the Revolution to be published in America, sister of James Otis, colonial patriot leader, and wife of James Warren, prominent Massachusetts statesman. When Mercy Warren's book appeared in 1805, the only other history of the Revolution in existence was the one published in England in 1788 by the Reverend William Gordon.

In the determination of the Federalists to see the Constitution ratified, Mercy Warren saw the "*dark, secret* and *profound intrigues*" of "rapacious" men bent on "growing rich by oppression" while the "philosophic lovers of freedom" wept.

"What have you been contending for these ten years past?" James Lincoln of South Carolina asked his fellow Americans. "Liberty!" he answered. But, "What is liberty? The power of governing yourselves. If you adopt this Constitution have you this power?"

From Maine to Georgia, from the Atlantic to the Mississippi, every Antifederalist answered, "No!"

Quickly supplied with a copy of the Constitution, the Congress, meeting in New York, quickly acted on it. Too quickly, said the Antifederalists. They saw in the speed with which Congress requested the states to call ratifying conventions a "deep and devious plot" by the Federalists to ram the Constitution down the throats of the people before their eyes could take it in and their minds comprehend what is said.

Major William Jackson, secretary of the Federal Convention, carried the Constitution to New York himself. On the twentieth of September it was on the floor of the Congress. On the twenty-sixth the debate began. It lasted only two days.

Of the thirty delegates present, ten had been members of the Federal Convention. Most of them had rushed up to New York to see to it that the document they had signed was acted on without delay.

Even so, the message that Congress sent to the states was bland to the point of saying nothing. It did not even contain the word "constitution." It merely asked the states to call conventions for the purpose of considering the recommendations voted by the late Federal Convention.

Not even the most ardent Federalist could say that the Confederation Congress had endorsed what many suspected would be its death warrant. All Congress had done was wash its hands of the problem by turning it over to the states.

Whereupon the battle of words, ideas, and blows began in dead earnest.

17

Uproar in Pennsylvania

PENNSYLVANIA MOVED FIRST.

Pro-Constitution men dominated its one-house legislature, the Assembly, that fall.

On the morning of Friday, September 28, one of them, George Clymer of Philadelphia, arose to offer a motion. Clymer himself was a Founding Father, having attended the Federal Convention. He proposed that elections be held at once for the purpose of naming delegates to a ratifying convention to begin in late November. Even as a second to his motion was heard, pandemonium took over.

Half a dozen men from the rural western counties of the state were on their feet protesting. All of them were either already Antifederalists or leaning that way.

William Findley of Fayette County did much of the talking. Fayette was frontier country then and Findley was every inch the frontiersman. Abundant brown hair fell to his shoulders. His lean face tightened as he spoke. Under thick shelf-like lashes his dark eyes flashed.

Why all the rush, Findley wanted to know. It was his guess that outside of the city of Philadelphia no more than twenty Pennsylvanians had laid eyes on the Constitution. Wait, Findley implored. Give the people time to read what the document said and digest it.

This session of the assembly was due to end at noon on the next day. Statewide elections during November would name the members of the next Assembly. Why not wait until then? Let the next Assembly decide whether or not Pennsylvania should call a convention to ratify the Constitution.

Wait! Findley said it again. Wait!

But wait was exactly what the pro-Constitution leaders of the Assembly did not want to do. They were in charge of this Assembly. They might not be in charge of the next one.

Findley and his friends fought valiantly for delay. But they fought against overwhelming odds. The most they could accomplish was to get the vote on Clymer's motion postponed until four o'clock that afternoon.

When four o'clock came it brought with it a shock for the Federalists. No quorum! Not enough men on the floor to cast a vote under the rules. A quick roll call revealed that all nineteen Antifederalist members had quietly slipped away.

The presiding officer ordered the sergeant at arms to find them and bring them in. When the sergeant at arms returned, he was alone. The missing assemblymen, he reported, had locked themselves into their lodgings at "Boyd's house on Sixth Street." He had yelled at them to come out and they had told him to go to a "hot place."

So he had returned to the Assembly, which for the rest of the afternoon was indeed a hot place. It was heated by the frustration of forty-five Federalists unable to vote for a ratifying convention because they were two persons short of having a quorum.

That night riotous crowds roamed Philadelphia's streets. Taverns resounded with arguing voices, varied at moments by the thud of fistfights.

Among the rioters were many of the city's skilled workers, its artisans and mechanics. These men favored the Constitution. They believed its adoption would improve trade with Europe and increase the demand for their skills.

Next morning a gang of them stoned the windows of Boyd's house on Sixth Street. They smashed the front door open, seized two of the Antifederalist assemblymen, and dragged them, fighting, to the State House. There, in the legislative hall, the two Antis were literally thrown into their seats, their bodies bruised, their clothing torn, their faces, according to a firsthand account, "white with rage."

Now there was a quorum. Now the lawmakers of Pennsylvania could vote on the motion to summon a ratifying convention.

The motion carried: forty-five for it, two against.

On November 21 the Pennsylvania ratifying convention opened at the State House in Philadelphia.

Day after day James Wilson was on his feet, extolling the advantages of the Constitution he had helped to write in this very building. The Scottish-born Philadelphia attorney and land speculator was not an imposing figure. His shoulders were narrow. His face, with its plump chin and little round cheeks, was plain. His half-moon glasses hung low on his stunted nose. His O-shaped eyes gazed out over them.

Wilson said very little about liberty and the rights of man. He said most men were driven by "self-interest." He said those Americans who thought they could make better livings under the Constitution favored it and those who thought otherwise did not. He chided what he called the "Antifeds" for claiming that the Constitution would destroy their freedoms when what they really meant was that it might hamper their business interests. He thought the "Feds" should be honest. They should come right out and say that under a strong central government, able to pay its debts and negotiate trade agreements with Europe, most Americans would find it easier to get rich.

Plain words from a mind that Dr. Benjamin Rush described as "a blaze of light." Listening to Wilson, many a farmer come to the convention from the western countries ready to vote against the Constitution, decided to vote for it.

After weeks of speechifying, the state of Pennsylvania ratified. The vote was forty-six to twenty-three.

There were celebrations. At the little frontier town of Carlisle the Federalists gathered in a grove of hemlock trees. Bonfires blazed, fireworks crackled, picnickers rimmed hastily carpentered tables laden with food.

Wilson was there. He had just started a scheduled speech when a mob of club-toting Antifeds charged into the area, oversetting tables and cracking skulls. A group of them pulled Wilson from the platform and hurled him to the ground. Not satisfied with subjecting the Philadelphian to this indignity, they rained blows on his prostrate body. Wilson, it was said later, would have been killed had not an old soldier thrown himself over the fallen man and taken the blows.

For all of the rush in Pennsylvania, that state did not have the honor of being the first to ratify. That went to little Delaware, and by the end of January five states in all had ratified, in the following order: Delaware, Pennsylvania, and New Jersey on the seventh, twelfth, and eighteenth of December 1787, Georgia and Connecticut on the second and eighth of January 1788.

As the New Year began, the eyes of the country turned northward, to Massachusetts, whose convention opened in Boston in early January. Massachusetts was the second largest state in the Union. Both sides were braced for a fight. Both knew that how Massachusetts went would have a profound effect on the thinking of people in those states that had not yet held their conventions.

18

Leadership Wins at Boston

Massachusetts did things in a big way. Early in January the 355 delegates elected to the state ratifying convention converged on Boston. Plans were to meet at the State House. But no chamber there was big enough. The convention moved to the Brattle Street Church. Its auditorium gave the delegates legroom. Its broad galleries accommodated a large daily influx of excited and often noisy spectators.

The Federalists fretted. Outside Boston and vicinity sentiment seemed to run strong against the Constitution. Twenty-one of the delegates had participated in Shays's Rebellion. These and many of the men coming from the western counties looked unkindly on a general government empowered to levy and collect taxes.

In much of Massachusetts the town-meeting tradition still prevailed. One village, Ashfield, viewed the weak Confederation as far too much government for any country. The people of Ashfield let it be known that they took orders only from God.

On the eve of the convention worried Federalists, counting heads as best they could, concluded that at least two hundred of the delegates were not in favor of the Constitution.

But before the convention was two weeks old, a startling fact was in view. The smallness of their numbers notwithstanding, the Federalists had one enormous advantage.

They had the leaders.

One of them was Rufus King. Stalwart in appearance, sharp of mind, well-educated, King would later move to New York and become a member of the first United States Senate. Still later, after the death of Alexander Hamilton, he would become the recognized leader of the country's first true political party, the Federalists.

Another strong Federalist delegate at Boston was Theophilus Parsons, billiant lawyer, compelling speaker.

Still another was Theodore Sedgwick, who hailed from the far-western reaches of the state.

All of the Federalist leaders at the Massachusetts convention were known and respected throughout the state and beyond. All were men of great intellectual force. More to the point, they worked together. All of them knew exactly what they wanted. No obstacle thrown in their path could make them lift their eyes from their goal. In the fiery vigor shown by the Federalists in the Great Debate over the Constitution one sees the inspired action of men convinced that they were the bearers of the future, of destiny. In their hands lay the responsibility for seeing to it that their country made the great leap from a gaggle of quarreling states to a united nation.

The Antifederalists of the Massachusetts convention could look for guidance to only two delegates of more than local fame. One was Samuel Adams, still revered as a major architect of the break with England. The other was John Hancock, richest merchant in the commonwealth and signer of the Declaration of Independence.

Neither contributed any real leadership: Adams, because he was uncertain in his mind as to what should be done about the Constitution; Hancock, because he was incapable of serving any cause until he was absolutely sure that it was going to win.

And on the eve of the convention Hancock was not sure. As he was the governor of the state, the first act of the convention was to elect him as its chairman. But it would be many days before Hancock occupied the chair of the presiding officer.

There was a report around town that he was "heart and soul" against the Constitution. Hancock knew of this report. He also knew that if he attended the convention the Antifederalist would look to him as their champion, and he had no intention of taking sides until he knew which way the wind was blowing. Instead of coming to the convention, he retired to his palatial home on Beacon Hill. His excuse (often used to duck unpleasant duties) was illness: an attack of gout, against which his obliging doctors wrapped him in bandages like an Egyptian mummy.

Elbridge Gerry, who had refused to sign the Constitution in Philadelphia, could have provided the Antis of the Massachusetts ratifying convention with forceful leadership. Gerry had a trenchant mind and persuasive ways. But after his return to his home state from Philadelphia he had rushed into print with a long list of criticisms of the Constitution. During the election of delegates to the ratifying convention, he offered himself as a candidate. Unfortunately for the cause he represented, Gerry lived in Federalist-dominated Boston. The citizens there were not about to vote for a man so conspicuously opposed to the adoption of the Constitution.

At the Brattle Street Church the Antis were aware of the weakness of their leadership. Soon after the convention began, they got permission for Gerry to sit in on the sessions as an unofficial consultant or adviser.

A good scheme, but it didn't work. As Gerry was not a

member of the convention, he could not ask for the floor. He could speak only when spoken to, and somehow the Antifederalists never got around to speaking to him. Day after day he sat there, his head bursting with arguments against the Constitution that he was never allowed to voice. With every passing hour the lines of worry in his thin grim face grew deeper. He took his irritation out on the cane propped between his knees, frequently biting at the head of it.

One day Gerry simply walked out. "In the high dudgeon," according to a Federalist delegate, delighted to see the Bay State's ablest Anti vanish from the scene.

Early in the course of the convention the great complaint of the Antifederalists arose: "There is no declaration of rights!"

This cry had come up in earlier conventions in other states. On those occasions the Federalists had met it by arguing that no bill of rights was needed in the national Constitution.

Now, in Boston, they met the challenge in another and more effective way. All right, they said in essence to their opponents, since you feel the Constitution needs some amendments, tell us what you think they should be. Put them in writing. Then adopt the Constitution as it now stands, and after it goes into effect, we will join with you to make certain that the amendments you desire are added to it.

It was a brilliant scheme. It would work at Boston, and later on it would work at the ratifying conventions in other states.

At Boston the Antifederalist bosses got busy at once, only to discover that it was easier to cry for a bill of rights than to frame one. Disagreements arose as to exactly what amendments they should propose. And while the Antis fussed among themselves, the Feds acted.

Meeting out-of-doors—privately, that is—the Federalist leaders drafted a series of possible amendments. Word of what they were doing spread fast. It started the members of the convention thinking. Many Antifederalist took the willingness of the Federalists to recommend amendments as a sign that the Constitution they were so determined to see adopted might not be such a bad thing after all.

Federalist Theophilus Parsons was a whole brain trust in himself. Suddenly Parsons came up with another stunning idea. What he suggested to his fellow Federalists went something like this:

"Let us not present these recommended amendments to the convention ourselves. Let us try to persuade the most popular man in Massachusetts, Governor Hancock, to do it for us."

The others nodded. Some of them chuckled to themselves.

They knew the character of Governor Hancock. He longed to be liked, to be popular. He yearned for the adulation of the crowds. He wanted to be on the winning side of every argument.

Yes, perhaps the Antifederalist governor could be persuaded to further the cause of Federalism.

One morning a committee called on the governor in his Beacon Hill mansion. Parsons was there, clutching in his hand a well-phrased speech he had written for the purpose of introducing the recommended amendments. Theodore Sedgwick was there. So was Sam Adams. The Federalists had invited him to come along.

It was Sam Adams who, on the eve of the Revolution, had won over John Hancock—and his fortune—to the patriot cause. Subsequently the two men had quarreled at times, but the older Adams still had much influence over the vain governor.

The governor greeted his visitors courteously, listened to them attentively, read the speech Parsons had written—and nodded.

On the morning of the thirtieth of January Hancock entered the auditorium of the Brattle Street Church, flaunting his white bandages and thrilled to the core by the cheers which arose as he marched down the aisle to take for the first time the presiding officer's chair to which the delegates had elected him.

From there he presented the recommended amendments (others drafted by Sam Adams would be considered later) and read Parson's speech. He took care to leave everyone under the impression that he, John Hancock, had framed the amendments and written the speech.

It was high moment for the Federalist. Henceforth the going would be easier for them.

On February 6, 1788, by a vote of 187 to 168, the commonwealth of Massachusetts ratified the federal Constitution.

It was the sixth state to do so.

Rapidly two other states followed suit: Maryland on the twenty-sixth of April by a vote of 63 to 11; South Carolina on the twenty-third of May by a vote of 149 to 73.

Then at one o'clock on the afternoon of June 21, 1788, the last fall of the gavel at the New Hampshire ratifying convention in the little town of Concord on the Merrimac River proclaimed the birth of the federal government. The vote at Concord was fifty-seven to forty-six.

Now the Constitution was in effect, the Union established. But, generally speaking, the Federalists were not jubilant. Under the terms of the Constitution itself, the nine states that had now endorsed it could go ahead and set up the government it called for. But how long could such a union last, the Federalists asked one another, if the important states of Virginia and New York were not a part of it? And neither of those states had as yet endorsed the Constitution, although the conventions of both states were underway. Virginia's delegates were meeting in the New Academy on Shockoe Hill in Richmond, New York's in the old stone courthouse in the little Hudson River town of Poughkeepsie.

Deep anxiety edged with hope ran through pro-Constitution circles as the Federalists of the rest of the country watched the proceedings at these places—for the gatherings at Richmond and Poughkeepsie were the hardest fought of all the ratifying conventions.

19

Storm over Richmond

VIRGINIA WAS THE LARGEST, THE MOST INFLUENTIAL state in the Union. Not yet had the Old Dominion transferred its western lands to Congress. The acres it ruled still stretched to the Mississippi, still included what are now the states of West Virginia and Kentucky. Within this vast region lived one-fifth of all of the inhabitants of America.

When on the second of June the state ratifying convention opened in the New Academy in Richmond, the 170 delegates ranged from finely attired planters from the Northern Neck (Washington's neighborhood) to frontiersmen in hunting shirts and coonskin hats. The delegates from beyond the mountains had come to the state capital through Indian country. Pistols hung at their sides, and the hard, scrappy life of the pioneer world was written on their lean faces and in their taut, watchful eyes.

Physically Washington was not there. He had not offered himself as a candidate during the election of delegates. But in spirit he was very much there. Everybody knew where the master of Mount Vernon stood. No American was more eager to see the Constitution in effect.

In Virginia, as in Massachusetts, the Federalists had reason to worry. It was commonly believed that more than half the delegates were ill disposed toward the Constitution. In Virginia, as in Massachusetts, the leaders of Federalism came to the convention primed for a hard fight, well organized and in perfect agreement as to what moves to make, what strategy to pursue.

Outstanding among them were Judge Edmund Pendleton of the state supreme court, Chancellor (top judge of the state) George Wythe; George Nicholas of Albemarle County, and, of course, Madison.

Elected chairman of the convention on the opening day, white-haired, sixty-seven-year-old Pendleton hobbled painfully on crutches to the platform. A recent fall from a horse had dislocated his hip. But so keen was the judge's mind, so well put his remarks, that his handicaps only added to the respect with which he was listened to.

Wythe was probably the finest of the country's lawyers. Small, erect, spry as a boy at sixty-two, he was best known as founder of the country's first academic department of law at William and Mary College in Williamsburg. Among his past students were Jefferson, still watching the progress of his country from France, and John Marshall, destined to be a Chief Justice of the United States, then a young lawyer and a delegate of the Virginia ratifying convention. Among Wythe's future students would be the great Henry Clay of Kentucky. Wythe, too, was often on the platform. He presided whenever the convention met as a Committee of the Whole. It did so much of the time.

Nicholas and Madison worked on the floor. Each in his way provided a rallying point for the pro-Constitution forces.

Even in a state noted for its orators, Nicholas stood out. He was a strange creature to look at, so fat that a cartoonist of the day pictured him as a giant prune on tiny legs. But when Nicholas spoke in his rich, rolling voice no one in the room, Federalist or Antifederalist, failed to pay attention.

Madison did not have Nicholas's bulk. He was so small that spectators in the galleries had to strain to see him when he rose. Sometimes he could attract the notice of the chair only by jumping up and down and waving his hands. Even so, he was everlastingly in action, speaking so earnestly and at such length that on several occasions he lost his voice. Once sheer exhuastion kept him to his lodgings for three days.

In a strikingly important way the convention in Richmond differed from the one five months earlier in Boston. Unlike the Bay State Antis the Virginia Antifederalists could not complain of a lack of leadership. Quite the contrary.

In the country as a whole most people though of Washington as the first citizen of the land. But within the borders of the Old Dominion he was generally regarded as only third or fourth on the totem pole. To most Virginians the top heroes of their commonwealth were Patrick Henry and George Mason, with the attractive young governor of the commonwealth, Edmund Randolph, running close behind them.

And as the convention opened in Richmond's New Academy, the report going the rounds was that all three—Henry, Mason, and Randolph—intended to see to it that the biggest and most powerful of the states became the first of them to refuse to ratify the Constitution.

A hush fell over the great hall of the Academy when, on the third day of the meeting, young Governor Randolph rose to utter his first remarks.

Everybody knew that Randolph had refused to sign the Constitution in Philadelphia. Everybody knew that one of his main objections was that the document put all the power of the presidency into the hands of one man. Everyone knew that Randolph believed that in time this provision would saddle the country with a king. A "fœtus of monarchy," he called it.

What everybody did not know—what hardly anyone knew—was that months before the opening of the convention Madison had written a carefully thought-out letter to Randolph. The two men were close. Madison knew that Randolph was wavering in his mind. He was beginning to think that his opposition to the Constitution might be a mistake.

In his letter Madison charged that Patrick Henry's demand for a bill of rights and a second Federal Convention did not express Henry's real thoughts. Behind Henry's repeated expressions of concern for the freedoms of the people lay a desire to keep Virginia out of the Union so that it and the other Southern states could form a separate confederation of their own.

A second federal convention, Madison wrote Randolph, would upset the good work of the first one and "give opportunities to designing men which might be impossible to counteract."

When Randolph spoke out for the first time at the Richmond convention, he had had six months to consider Madison's statements. To some extent he had come to agree with them. He said as much to the other delegates and to the spectators filling the galleries of the great hall of the Academy.

When he sat down there was another and longer hush. It took his listeners a little time to take in what he had said.

Governor Randolph had changed his mind. He planned to support the Constitution.

Patrick Henry was the first of the Antis to recover enough from the shock to speak up.

Within the borders of the Old Dominion Henry was still lovingly remembered as the young lawyer from the back country who, on the eve of the war, fueled the flames of patriotism everywhere with his ringing "Give me liberty or death!" For three years he had served as the governor of Virginia.

At fifty-two he was tall, thin, and slightly stooped. His face was long and thin and sloping. Blue eyes brooded behind round spectacles. He dressed carelessly. The brown wig mashing his reddish hair was ill-fitting. Often, speaking on the floor, he emphasized his points by snatching the wig from his head and whirling it aloft.

He whirled it now and glared at his long-time friend and onetime political ally, Edmund Randolph.

"Strange and unaccountable." Thus Henry described Randolph's change of mind. He suggested that Randolph had been keeping bad company. Someone "of great influence" had lured him into the camp of the enemy. He hinted that the influential enemy had promised Randolph some sort of future political advancement.

Everybody assumed that the bad company Henry had in mind was Washington. Some suspected Madison as well.

Randolph waited a few days before he replied. Then be blazed. Henry, he declared, had accused him of "inconsistency," and had questioned his honesty. There was more. The two men traded insults and that evening Henry sent a friend to hand Randolph a challenge.

For several days Richmond gossip bubbled with the possibility of a duel between the present governor and the former governor. Idle chatter. No duel ensued. Somehow the two men were persuaded to cool down, even to treat one another civilly again.

But their heated exchange set the tone of the Virginia convention. It was a long, rough battle. And a wordy one.

On the Antifederalist side most of the words came from Patrick Henry. Henry had no equal as an orator. He did not offer his listeners facts and reason in the manner of Madison, Pendleton, and Nicholas. He gave them passion and poetry, the heart-stopping performance one expects of a great actor on the stage.

How he moved them! They could listen to him all day. Once they did, and Henry would have spoken for another day had not the rumble and crackle of a sudden thunderstorm in the skies over Richmond blotted out his words and forced him to desist. Then and there a saying was born: "Only God can silence Patrick Henry."

The Constitution, Henry thundered, "is as radical as the

resolution which separated us from Great Britain . . . The rights of conscience, trial by jury, liberty of the press, all your communities and franchises, all pretensions to human rights . . . are rendered insecure, if not lost, by this change . . . Is this tame relinquishment of rights worthy of free-men? . . . It is said eight states have adopted this plan. I declare that if twelve states and a half had adopted it, I would with manly firmness, and in spite of an erring world, reject it . . . Liberty, greatest of all earthly blessings—give us that precious jewel, and you may take every thing else!"
Madison, Pendleton, and Nicholas strove to answer Henry. Madison noted that the opponents of the Constitution feared it would give the country a general government so strong the state governments would wither away.

Not so, said Madison. The general government would only be powerful enough to take care of the affairs of the country as a whole. The states would still have more than enough power to control their local affairs. The Antis spoke of the proposed new government as "consolidated." It wasn't, said Madison. It was "federal." It was "of a mixed nature," he explained, adding that "it was in a manner unprecedented." He urged the delegates to consider the Constitution "with open minds." He hoped they would not try to compare it with anything else, because nothing quite like it had ever before been created.

Swinging on his crutches, Judge Pendleton took issue with Henry's repeated assertion that the government out-lined by the Constitution would curb the freedoms of the people.

"There is no quarrel between government and liberty," the old judge declared. "The former is the shield and pro-tector of the latter. The war is between government and licentiousness, faction, turbulence, and other violations of the rules of society, to preserve liberty." Was not the his-tory of the Confederation one long story of quarrels be-tween the states and disorders within them? Did not the Constitution promise to bring peace and order? And if it failed to do so, no harm—the people had made the Consti-tution; the people could correct it.

At Richmond as at Boston both sides agreed that the Constitution needed a bill of rights. At Richmond, however, the quarrel over when was fiercer and more prolonged.

The Antis wanted the bill of rights added now. They wanted to postpone adoption of the Constitution until all the other states agreed to the added amendments.

The Feds protested. They pointed out that many of the states already had ratified the Constitution as written. Under the procedure suggested by the Antis, those states would have to hold their ratifying conventions all over again. That might take forever. Adopt the Constitution as it is, the Feds pleaded. Add the bill of rights later.

"Previous amendments," cried the Antis. "Subsequent amendments," cried the Feds.

On June 24 Chancellor Wythe moved that the Constitution be adopted "with subsequent amendments." Wythe acted just in time. The Antis had been planning, later that day, to move for adoption on the basis of "previous amendments."

The debate on Wythe's motion was still going on at adjournment time that afternoon. Shortly after it resumed the next morning, Madison rose to say something that would be long remembered. Straining to make himself heard, for his weak voice was all but gone, he announced that after the Constitution took effect he would "work for a bill of rights."

It would be said later that Madison's promise that morning won converts to the Federalist cause.

The end came suddenly. About an hour later, by a vote of eighty-nine to seventy-nine, Virginia became the tenth state to ratify the Constitution.

20

Governor Clinton Takes a Walk

A MESSENGER ON FREQUENTLY CHANGED FAST HORSES
sped the news of Virginia's decision northward. When, on
the second of July, he reached Poughkeepsie, the sixty-five
delegates to the New York convention, meeting in the stone
courthouse there, were in the sixteenth day of a debate that
would continue for almost another month with never a dull
moment.

The argument at Poughkeepsie ran the same course as
the argument in Richmond—with one big difference.

At Richmond the Antis fought for previous amendments.
At Poughkeepsie they fought for the passage of a two-
headed resolution. Under one of its provisions the Constitution would not be allowed to take effect until after the
holding of a second federal convention. Under the other
provision this second convention would frame a series of
amendments. These would be designed for the most part
to strip the federal government of many of the powers assigned to it by the Constitution as written in Philadelphia.

"Previous amendments!" was the Antifederalists' war cry in Richmond.

"A second convention!" was their cry in Poughkeepsie.

George Washington once described the framing of the Constitution in Philadelphia as a "miracle." Certainly that word can be applied to what happened at the New York ratifying convention. When its sixty-five delegates began their work on June 17, the Antifederalist majority was so overwhelming that there was every reason to believe that the Empire State would reject the Constitution. When they completed it forty-one days later, the tables had turned.

As the major Federalist leader, Alexander Hamilton contributed much to the miracle. Events happening miles away from Poughkeepsie contributed even more.

In the beginning the New York convention was Governor Clinton's show. Named chairman of the convention on opening day, that pillar of Antifederalism had the satisfaction of knowing that at least two-thirds of the sixty-four men seated before him were on his side.

Almost all the nineteen Federalist delegates came from New York City and vicinity. Beyond the outskirts of the big city the Constitution had few friends in New York State. Divided on many issues, the manor lords along the eastern banks of the Hudson and the small farmers on the other side were in accord on this one. As things stood, they paid little or no taxes. Much of the money needed by the state government came from taxes (duties) paid by citizens of New Jersey and Connecticut on imported goods coming to them through the harbor of New York City. Were the Constitution adopted, only the federal government could collect such duties. Then the manor lords and the farmers would have to start digging into their own pockets to support their state government.

No one was more aware of all this than Clinton. No one was more eager to see things kept as much as possible the way they were now.

Clinton had won fights before. He looked forward to winning this one. In the art of politics, early-American-style, he had no superiors and few equals. He had governed the state of New York for eleven years. He would be its governor for another ten in all.

His devoted followers were fond of saying, "The Old Man has the state in his pocket." To which the local wags were fond of adding, "And don't try to find out which pocket it's in, because what the Old Man doesn't want you to find out, you won't."

In the summer of 1788 the Old Man wasn't really all that old. Forty-nine, with a short but powerful body, a large plain face, under jutting eyelashes, he had the clear and open eyes of a man who knew where he was going and how to get there.

Blandly, with a hand accustomed to the gavel, he brought the New York convention to order. He would speak little during the next forty-one days. There was no need for him to talk. Out on the floor sat a man well equipped to talk for the Antifederalist majority.

This was Melancton Smith. A big man in his mid-fifties, Smith was rough all over. His face was broad and raw-looking, his body muscular. Within this human fortress a splendid mind worked. No formal schooling fueled it. Smith had educated himself, and no man ever had a better teacher. Born to a poor family in Jamaica, Long Island, he had made of himself a prosperous lawyer and merchant in New York City. He came to the convention as a delegate from Dutchess County (Poughkeepsie was the county seat), where he owned and farmed extensive lands.

Smith was a moderate. He did not share the belief of some of his followers at Poughkeepsie that the Federal Convention was a plot by the country's aristocrats to take all power of the country into their own hands. He had long ago decided that the Confederation needed strengthening. But at Philadelphia, he argued, the Founding Fathers had gone too far.

The Articles of Confederation, Smith recalled, had placed the state legislatures between the Congress and the people to protect the people. "We were then," he went on, ". . . too cautious . . . But now it is proposed to go into the contrary, and a more dangerous extreme; to remove all barriers, to give the new government free access to our pockets and ample command of our persons, and that without providing for a genuine and fair representation of the people.''

Robert R. Livingston was one of the first to speak for the other side. Forty-two-year-old Livingston was the chancellor of the state and one of the few manor lords to support the Constitution. Thick dark curls tumbled down his imposing forehead, his dark eyes twinkled easily, and he had the strong, prominent nose common to the males of his large and influential family.

The Confederation, Livingston said, was "a riddle." Some people thought it a real government and some thought it just a creature of the states. Now here was the federal Constitution. It proposed a national government whose supremacy over the states was clear to everyone.

"There is your choice, gentlemen," the chancellor concluded in essence. "A vote against the Constitution is a vote for mystery and nonsense. A vote for it is a vote for clarity and sense."

Livingston's speech amused the Antifederalists, but it did not change their minds. Even after word arrived that New Hampshire had ratified and that the Constitution was legally in effect, New York's Antis stood their ground. How long could the Union last, they asked one another, with powerful Virginia outside it?

Then came the news that Virginia was in. On top of that came another development, even more alarming to the foes of the Constitution. Up the Hudson River came reports that if the Poughkeepsie convention refused to ratify, the city of New York would break away from the state, hold its own convention, and join the Union.

Governor Clinton was noticeably jolted. Early one morning the Old Man was seen walking by himself on the porch—the piazza—of the courthouse. Back and forth he paced. On his face was the drawn expression of a man struggling with inner doubts. When he returned to the chair of the presiding officer, there was an air of listlessness about him. Some took it to be the air of a man who had given up the fight.

Quick to notice that the opposition was weakening, Hamilton delivered one of the most effective speeches of his career. Clause by clause he went through the Constitution, striving to show the Antifederalist that their fears concerning it were groundless.

Listening attentively, Melancton Smith, as he admitted later, was impressed by some of Hamilton's arguments. It was the Antifederalist leader himself who offered the motion that brought the long convention to an end. On Saturday, July 24, Smith moved that the delegates endorse the Constitution as written. On Monday, July 26, they did so. The vote was breathtakingly close, thirty to twenty-seven.

Now eleven states had ratified the Constitution, and it was everywhere assumed that in time the remaining two, North Carolina and Rhode Island, would come around.

In time they did: North Carolina, after two stormy conventions, by a vote of ninety-four to seventy-seven on November 21, 1789; Rhode Island, belatedly and grudgingly, by a vote of thirty-four to thirty-two on May 29, 1790.

21

The Federal Procession, the Bill of Rights, the Endless Debate

AMERICANS EVERYWHERE CELEBRATED THE ADOPTION OF the Constitution.

In every city cheering throngs poured into the streets to watch parades gaudy with brightly colored floats and listen to excited and exciting orators. For years to come these festivals would be remembered, collectively, as the Federal Procession of 1788.

None was more lavish than Philadelphia's. The Quaker City chose to stage its procession on the Fourth of July, thus commemorating at one and the same time the birth of the country and the birth of the federal government.

At dawn of the great day a peal of bells rang out from the steeple of Christ Church. Simultaneously the cannons boomed from the ship *Rising Sun*, anchored at the foot of Market Street. Along the waterfront, from South Street to the suburb called Northern Liberties, ten other vessels faced the shore. Each carried on its masthead a huge white flag bearing the name of one of the ten states that had ratified

167

to date: *Pennsylvania . . . Massachusetts . . . New Hampshire* . . . All day a lively breeze bathed the city. All day the pennants on the ships along the waterfront fluttered in it.

At eight in the morning the procession itself began taking form. At nine-thirty it moved. A mile and a half long it was, headed by the First City Troop of Light Dragoons, their white jackets edged with red, their white saddlecloths with blue.

Behind them came citizens on elaborately caparisoned horses or imaginatively designed floats, bearing a profusion of symbols—some to honor the French armies and navies that had helped the Americans to win their Revolution; some to commemorate the treaty of peace of 1783; some to express in a great variety of ways the widespread feeling that a new and better era had dawned for the republic.

Band after band came by, blaring the music of an ode written for the occasion by Francis Hopkinson, chairman of the committee of arrangements, local poet, wit, and jurist. The paraders and the spectators sang it together!

> Hail to this festival!—all hail the day!
> Columbia's standard on her roof display!
> And let the people's motto ever be,
> "United thus, and thus united, free!"

Group after group marched by, representing every facet of the city's life: it merchants, its manufacturers, its workers. The carpenters and the bricklayers marched together. The banner snaking in the breeze above them carried this motto: *Both the Buildings and the Rulers are the Works of Our Hands*. On a stage drawn by four strapping horses stood a complete printing plant. It was the display of the makers and sellers of books. Its motto: *We Protect and Are Supported by Liberty*.

Largest and most impressive of the horse-drawn floats was the one carrying a building identified as the "Fœderal Edifice." Its ten finished pillars symbolized the states that had ratified, its unfinished three those that would do so later.

Slowly but steadily the huge procession moved forward—to a section of the Commons newly named the Federal Green. Here the speeches were listened to and applauded. From here, as the evening light withdrew, seventeen thousand Philadelphians scattered to their homes.

Dr. Benjamin Rush, himself one of the speakers, could hardly believe what his eye beheld. Such joy in the people's faces, such exultation. So mammoth was the crowd, so wild its cheering, that the doctor could only assume that both the city's Federalists and Antifederalists had turned out. Having fought the good fight, both stood ready to give the new Constitution and the government it proposed a chance.

"Now it is done," the happy doctor said. "Now we are a nation!"

Indeed, the nation was beginning. Months before Rhode Island became the thirteenth and last state to ratify the Constitution, the government it called for began operation.

In the spring of 1789 the members of the first Congress under the Constitution gathered on the second floor of Federal Hall in New York City to begin their work. On April 30, on the little balcony at the front of that building, Washington placed his hand on a Bible, borrowed at the last moment from a nearby Masonic Lodge, to become the first President. And a few weeks later Congress put underway the judiciary branch of the new government, the Supreme Court, headed by John Jay of New York, with the title of Chief Justice of the United States.

Madison was one of the ten Virginians elected to the first House of Representatives. No one in American had forgotten his promise that once the Constitution was accepted he would work for a bill of rights. Madison had not forgotten, either. He was the prime mover in those actions, begun by the first Congress, that had the effect, toward the close of 1791, of adding to the Constitution its first ten amendments, the Bill of Rights.

At that point, in a sense, the great debate ended. In another sense it was just beginning.

Would the Constitution provide too strong a government? Too weak a government? Would it help the American people in their long effort to achieve the aims of their Revolution? Or would it halt that effort forever? Would it survive the attacks on it by those who hated the slavery compromise and who because of its presence in the Constitution labeled that document "a pact with death and a covenant with hell"? Would it survive the Civil War and the giant changes that came in its wake? Would it survive world wars abroad and harsh upheavals at home?

On, on, and on the great debate would go, as the heirs of the Founding Fathers struggled to make their Constitution work.

Washington once called the beginnings of this endless debate—the arguments in the state ratifying conventions—the best thing that ever happened to the American people.

It provided them with a school of political science, a course in the difficult arts of popular government.

Washington expressed the hope that whatever knowledge the people of his day had acquired in this manner they would hand down to their children and their children to theirs.

They would. The history of every nation is a conveyor belt along which the lessons learned by one generation, good or bad, pass on to the next. The American past has many tongues which, listened to, can inform and assist the present.

BIBLIOGRAPHY

"Anecdote of the Federal Convention of 1787," *The Living Age*, vol. 25 (May 18, 1850), pp. 357–59.

Bowen, Catherine Drinker. *Miracle at Philadelphia*, 1966.

Brant, Irving. *James Madison: Father of the Constitution, 1787–1800*. 1950.

———. *James Madison, The Nationalist, 1780–87*, 1948.

———. *James Madison, The Virginia Revolutionist*, 1941.

Corning, Amos E. *The Story of the Hasbrouck House, Washington's Headquarters, Newburgh, New York*, 1950.

The Delegate from New York, or, Proceedings of the Federal Convention of 1787; from the notes of John Lansing, Jr., Joseph R. Strayer, ed., 1939.

De Pauw, Linda. *The Eleventh Pillar: New York State and the Federal Constitution*, 1966.

Dunbar, Louise B. *A Study of "Monarchial" Tendencies in the United States from 1776 to 1801*, 1922.

Elliot, Jonathan. *The Debates in the Several State Conventions on the Adoption of the Federal Constitution . . . together with the Journal of the Federal Convention*, 5 vols., 1907.

Ferguson, Elmer James. *The Power of the Purse*, 1961.

Flexner, James Thomas. *George Washington in the American Revolution*, 1967.

Foner, Eric. *Tom Paine and Revolutionary America*, 1976.

Ford, Paul Leicester, ed. *Pamphlets on the Constitution of the United States: Published During Its Discussion by the People 1787–1788*, 1888.

Hawke, David Freeman. *Honorable Treason: The Declaration of Independence and the Men Who Signed It*, 1976.

Henderson, Herbert James. *Party Politics in the Continental Congress*, 1974.

Hendrick, Burton J. *The Lees of Virginia: Biography of a Family*, 1935.

Jackson, Joseph. *Encyclopedia of Philadelphia*, 4 vols., 1933.

Jensen, Merrill. *The Articles of Confederation: An Interpretation of the Social-Constitutional History of the American Revolution 1774–1781*, 1940.

Lynd, Staughton. *Class Conflict, Slavery and the United States Constitution: Ten essays*, 1967.

McDonald, Forrest. *E Pluribus Unum: The Formation of the American Republic*, 1965.

———. *We the People*, 1976.

Main, Jackson Turner. *The Antifederalists: Critics of the Constitution, 1781–1788*, 1961.

Minot, George Richards. *The History of Insurrections in Massachusetts in the Year Seventeen Hundred and Eighty Six and the Rebellion Consequent Thereon*, 1810.

Morris, Richard B. *The Peacemakers: The Great Powers and American Independence*, 1965.

Notes of Debates in the Federal Convention of 1787 Reported by James Madison, Adrienne Koch, ed., 1969.

"Notes of Major William Pierce on the Federal Convention of 1787," *American Historical Review*, vol. 3, pp. 310–34.

Roche, John P. "The Founding Fathers: A Reform Caucus in Action," *American Political Science Review*, vol. 55 (December 1961), pp. 799–816.

Rutland, Robert Allen. *The Ordeal of the Constitution: the Antifederalists and the Ratification Struggle of 1787–1788*, 1966.

Shaw, Samuel. *Journals*, 1847.

Tebbel, John. *George Washington's America*, 1954.

Van Doren, Carl. *The Great Rehearsal: The story of the making and ratifying of the Constitution of the United States*, 1948.

Warren, Joseph Parker. "The Confederation and Shays' Rebellion," *American Historical Review*, vol. 11, pp. 42–67.

Wills, Garry. *Inventing America: Jefferson's Declaration of Independence*, 1978.

Wood, Gordon S. *The Creation of the American Republic 1776–1787*, 1969.

———, ed. *Confederation and the Constitution: the Critical Issues*, 1973.

INDEX

About the Author

MILTON LOMASK has written eight books on the Revolutionary period, the most recent of which are AARON BURR: The Years from Princeton to Vice-President, THE FIRST AMERICAN REVOLUTION, and ODD DESTINY A Life of Alexander Hamilton. Mr. Lomask lives in McLean, Virginia.